"*How to Blog a Book* is a compact yet comprehensive guide to writing, publishing, and promotion that will empower writers to do their best work, get it published online and off, and make it successful."

MICHAEL LARSEN, literary agent (www.LarsenPomada.com) and co-director of the San Francisco Writers Conference

"If you dread the thought of starting or maintaining a blog, and balancing it with the stresses of writing a book, *How to Blog a Book* could well be the most valuable book you've discovered this year. Nina Amir gives you a toolbox of shortcuts, tricks, and workarounds that will save you money, time, and sanity. Follow her easy-to-understand guide (even for nontechies!), and you'll create a blog your fans love and a book that they'll promote for you."

JOAN STEWART, founder of The Publicity Hound (PublicityHound.com)

"Nina Amir shows you—no, actually implores you—to write your book on your blog in a painless, effortless way. Learn 'how' and 'why' you 'can' and 'should' write your book from your blog posts. *How to Blog a Book Revised and Expanded Edition* provides the road map to go from publishing a blog to publishing *your book*."

SCOTT LORENZ, Westwind Communications Book Marketing (Book-Marketing-Expert.com)

"If you're wondering how you are going to bend time to build your platform and write a book, wonder no more—you can do both. Nina Amir shows you how in this inspiring step-by-step book with easy-to-follow procedures, actionable tasks, tips, and technology recommendations. Even if you don't plan to blog a book, the material empowers you to author a more effective blog and streamline your writing process. Bets are you'll end up with a book after all."

CARLA KING, founder of Self-Pub Boot Camp (SelfPubBootCamp.com)

"*Blook* is a common publishing term where a writer creates a book from blog posts. Nina Amir provides the step-by-step wisdom to show any writer how to pull it off. Get this valuable resource."

W. TERRY WHALIN, author of *Jumpstart Your Publishing Dreams* and more than sixty books, and acquisitions editor at Morgan James Publishing

"I look at myself as a blogger, not a writer, but with Nina's book I now have a formula for writing that book! *How to Blog a Book* provides a simple process for turning your blog content into a book, and Nina does an excellent job of breaking the process into simple steps that anyone can follow."

IAN CLEARY, founder of www.RazorSocial.com

"Whether you plan to consciously blog a full-length book from start to finish, repurpose existing blog content into a book, or blog multiple series and turn the posts into e-books, *How to Blog a Book* has all the information you'll ever need to accomplish your goal. It's a book on blogging for authors and on authorship for bloggers."

PENNY C. SANSEVIERI, CEO of Author Marketing Experts, Inc. and adjunct professor at New York University (www.AMarketingExpert.com)

"Recycling your blog posts into a book may provide the easiest way to write a book, and *How to Blog a Book* provides the plan for producing both the blog and a book that agents, publishers, and readers will notice."
> **DAN POYNTER,** author of *The Self-Publishing Manual* and *How to Write Nonfiction* (www.ParaPublishing.com)

"Check out *How to Blog a Book*. It covers all the stops along the way to your destination as a published author."
> **JOHN KREMER,** author of *1001 Ways to Market Your Book* (www.Book Market.com)

"The old saying 'kill two birds with one stone' is the perfect metaphor for what Nina teaches in this valuable book. Blogging with the intention of turning the accumulated material into a complete trade book is a brilliant concept."
> **JEFF HERMAN,** literary agent (www.JeffHerman.com)

"Today writers have to think outside the box when it comes to getting their book ideas published. Blogging a book offers a unique way not only to attract readers but to catch the eyes of acquisitions editors—just what every aspiring author wants and needs to sell books."
> **JILL LUBLIN,** co-author of *Guerrilla Publicity* and author of *Get Noticed, Get Referrals* and *Networking Magic* (www.JillLublin.com)

"Turning your blog posts into a book is a terrific way to write your book and build your audience at the same time. Nina Amir will guide you through every step with practical advice based on real-world experience."
> **DANA LYNN SMITH,** author of the Savvy Book Marketer series of marketing guides for authors (www.SavvyBookMarketer.com)

"I believe that blogging can change your life. I also believe that writing a book is one of the achievements you will be most proud of. Combining the two can be a brilliant way to get the project moving. Nina's book will help you organize the process so you can put all your time and energy into writing and building a community."
> **JOANNA PENN,** author and blogger at *The Creative Penn*, voted one of the Top 10 Blogs for Writers (www.TheCreativePenn.com)

"If you are just starting out as a blogger, or if you already have 15,000 posts online, Nina Amir's *How to Blog a Book* has the plan for you. You can't go wrong with this book. Written to provide you with the easiest path from screen to page, *How to Blog a Book* gets you there while helping you dodge pitfalls and common frustrations. Read it and learn."
> **SHANE BIRLEY,** co-author of *Blogging for Dummies* (www.shanesworld.ca)

http://howtoblogabook.com

HOW TO BLOG A BOOK

REVISED & EXPANDED EDITION

write, publish, and promote your work
one post at a time

WRITER'S DIGEST
BOOKS

WritersDigest.***com***
Cincinnati, Ohio

NINA AMIR
Foreword by Joel Friedlander

For more resources for writers, visit www.writersdigest.com.

19 18   5 4

Distributed in Canada by Fraser Direct
100 Armstrong Avenue
Georgetown, Ontario, Canada L7G 5S4
Tel: (905) 877-4411

Distributed in the U.K. and Europe by F&W Media International
Brunel House, Newton Abbot, Devon, TQ12 4PU, England
Tel: (+44) 1626-323200, Fax: (+44) 1626-323319
E-mail: postmaster@davidandcharles.co.uk

Distributed in Australia by Capricorn Link
P.O. Box 704, Windsor, NSW 2756 Australia
Tel: (02) 4577-3555

ISBN-13: 978-1-59963-890-4

Edited by **Rachel Randall**
Designed by **Bethany Rainbolt, Alexis Brown, and Claudean Wheeler**
Production coordinated by **Debbie Thomas**

DEDICATION

To all *aspiring* authors and bloggers who would like to become *published* authors.

And to the late Professor John Keats, who said, "If you can write an article, you can write a nonfiction book. A nonfiction book is just a series of articles on the same topic strung together." I strung a series of related blog posts together instead. I hope you're proud, JK.

ACKNOWLEDGMENTS

First, I'd like to thank Michael Larsen and Elizabeth Pomada for including me as a panelist at the San Francisco Writers Conference. From that opportunity the *How to Blog a Book* blog was born. Second, my webmaster and blogmaster Linda Lee offered support and counsel. Third, Verna Dreisbach saw the entire "me" and a path to help me succeed.

Shane Birley, Linda Lee, Bill Belew, Robert Peters, Joel Friedlander, Jeff Herring, and MaAnna Stephenson served as consultants on the chapters containing technical information. Sue Collier and Carla King also lent their expertise to the section on self-publishing. Intellectual property attorneys Robert Pimm and Gary K. Marshall reviewed and added to the section on copyright.

At Writer's Digest Books, I'd like to thank Phil Sexton, my publisher and colleague; I am forever grateful to him for taking a risk on this book and on me. Thanks also to Rachel Randall, Bethany Rainbolt, and Debbie Thomas for supporting all my editorial and design needs.

I'd also like to thank my blog readers, who helped me become a published author, and the continuous flow of readers of the published book who made this second edition possible.

I'm extremely grateful to my husband, Ron—once upon a time my only blog reader. Every blogger needs a first reader. And each writer needs a supporter, an advocate, and a listening ear. Ron has been all of these and more. Without him, I wouldn't be able to pursue my writing and blogging.

I want to thank my mother for encouraging my creative bent for all these years. Here's a book that's not *bubkes*, Mom!

Last, but not least, huge heaps of gratitude to Karen Stone, my best friend. If I couldn't have shared this journey with her, it would have been awfully lonely.

http://howtoblogabook.com

FOREWORD

Since the publication of *How to Blog a Book* in 2012, both sides of the equation it presents—blogging and book publishing—have changed.

Blogging, frequently seen as a hobby, an obsession, or a duty imposed on you by your company, your publisher, or your social media consultant, has continued to grow. Where bloggers in earlier days were often treated as the illegitimate offspring of "real" media, the attractions of blogging remain strong, probably because blogging is the most democratic form of self expression ever invented. And as Nina Amir has shown, it's a platform with a multitude of benefits for writers who want to be successful.

Plenty of pundits have predicted the "death" of blogging, because there were so many millions of people starting blogs it became impossible to catalog or even count them. But blogging continued to morph into new forms, incorporating multimedia, penetrating other social media platforms, and claiming a seat at the table. It's common now to see bloggers sitting on panels on broadcast news, and they are quoted everywhere.

Blogs, in fact, are now the *most trusted source of information* for many consumers. Even people who profess to not read blogs are probably reading plenty of them; they just don't know it. They're likely reading online articles on blog sites that don't even call themselves "blogs" any more. We now get much of our information from blogs that go by "resource centers" or "information archives" or any number of other labels.

On the other end of the equation, book publishing has continued to evolve toward a future of which no one is quite certain. E-books, with their new financial models, present unique opportunities to publishers and authors. And author-controlled independent publishing has proven that it will be an increasingly important route for authors of all kinds to take to publication.

But even though blogs are written by writers—and books are, too—bloggers had little idea of the great advantages of publishing their own books.

In the indie publishing world, writers know they can establish authority, expand their networks, and monetize the secondary effects of publishing a book.

In the blogging world, bloggers know they can build a community of interest around their topic, network with other, bigger bloggers, and eventually find some way to monetize all this activity.

Are these two groups so different?

Even as *How to Blog a Book* was being published and Nina Amir was attempting to show writers how powerful a blog could be for their publishing plans, bloggers were just waking up to this thing called the Kindle.

At the time, I wrote on Copyblogger that "no group of people is better situated than bloggers RIGHT NOW to take advantage of the historic movement to digital books and the exploding popularity of self-publishing."[1]

Soon, Internet marketing, an activity most bloggers learn about if they survive the first few years online, started to wake up to book publishing, too. Especially the speed and ease of digital publishing.

And slowly, bloggers started using the content they had developed to publish real, honest-to-goodness books, not just PDFs formatted to look good on screen.

Authors, with the help of leaders in the indie publishing field—most notably Nina Amir—began to show authors how to use this wonderful blogging platform to create the books they had always wanted to write.

The ability to use blogging as a way to build authority, gather a community of interested readers, and cultivate a cadre of committed fans who will help in book launches and ongoing promotion has become important for all kinds of authors, not just those who choose self-publishing. Traditional publishers are leaving more and more of the responsibility for marketing books to the authors themselves.

---

1. www.copyblogger.com/blog-archive-ebooks

Savvy authors will make use of the advice in *How to Blog a Book* to provide the kind of high-engagement promotion at which blogs excel.

How to Blog a Book has helped countless authors plan, create, and publish books that might otherwise have remained ideas floating around in their minds.

By explaining the process, Nina put a powerful tool in writers' hands. And by repeatedly demonstrating, with her own blogging and publishing success, the effectiveness of the method, she has created a resource that will continue to help authors and bloggers for years to come.

This update to the original 2012 edition reflects many of the changes that have taken place in the intervening years, ensuring that *How to Blog a Book* is as relevant today as when it was first published.

For writers who have wondered about the role of blogging in their career, for writers who want to write books but don't want to tackle such a long document, for writers who dream of landing a traditional publishing deal, and for writers who understand that in the age of digital publishing every author is a *start-up business* trying to find room in a crowded marketplace, this book will be a lifeline.

Let Nina show you how these two powerful media tools—blogging and book publishing—can meld into publishing and platform success that benefits all your roles as a writer.

Joel Friedlander
San Rafael
January 2015

INTRODUCTION

WHY I STARTED A BLOG ABOUT HOW TO BLOG A BOOK

In January 2009 I started a blog about how to blog a book. At that time I had way too many unfinished nonfiction book projects—at least seven or eight. Though my expertise lies in nonfiction books, I also had one novel manuscript tucked away in a file on my computer.

So why did I begin a blog that forced me to initiate another book project? Why did I want to write a book in the public eye, where anyone could see whether I made progress, whether I finished it, and what my rough draft looked like?

I did it because blogging a book represents a great idea. Not only does blogging offer one of the quickest and easiest ways to write a book, blogging technology allows aspiring authors to promote themselves and their books as they write. This means writers build a following of readers as they blog their books into existence—a following of readers who also will buy a printed book based on those very same blog posts.

Why not simply write a book the old-fashioned way and publish it traditionally or independently instead? Today you must be more creative if you want to produce successful books, by which I mean books that sell to an above-average number of readers. You have to take your career into your own hands. You have to become your own public-relations representative and promotion and marketing director. You have to start your own publishing company. Taking advantage of the current online technology allows you to do these things easily and inexpensively, if not effortlessly.

Also, current technology has changed how people read. We live in the Internet Age. Many of us spend much of our day connected to the World Wide Web. We also read online. Why not write and publish online, too?

While other forms of publishing cost money, blogging your book is free—or can be. You can "publish" your book one post at a time on the Internet for nothing. Zero. Zilch. Or next to zilch, if you so choose.

Plus, if you write effective marketing copy and promote your blog well, it's possible to gain more readers than you would with a traditionally published book. Imagine one hundred, one thousand, ten thousand, or even one hundred thousand people a day reading your blog. Wouldn't you find that rewarding and exciting? Wouldn't you feel successful as an author?

Nowadays, blogs constitute one of the best ways to build the coveted author's platform. A blog read by thousands of people each month goes a long way toward impressing upon a publisher that you are a good publishing partner with a marketable idea. It also proves that you will be able to sell your independently published book. Many publishers now expect aspiring authors to have blogs and to blog often because this tool is so effective for creating successful books.

It behooves aspiring authors, therefore, to become bloggers—and to consider writing their books on their blogs.

CHAPTER 1

BOOK BLOGGING BASICS

As you read this book, agents and acquisitions editors are scanning the Internet to find new writers with great ideas to turn into books. Where do they find them? In the blogosphere—that place where bloggers write and blogs are published, read, and commented on by all sorts of readers.

Publishers Marketplace estimates that more than fifty blogs landed book deals in 2009 alone—and some other industry experts say sixty. However, the database produced by *Publishers Marketplace*, a publication that provides membership information for publishing professionals, includes only *announced* deals. We can safely assume that if announced and unannounced deals for that year were added together, the total number of contracts handed out by publishers to bloggers might be much larger. Although 2009 may have marked the height of the blog-to-book craze, the trend continues upward. *Publishers Marketplace* has released no new statistics for the years following the first burst that occurred from about 2003 to 2009, but a steady flow of blog-to-book success stories continues to surface. Based on information gathered from Google Alerts for the keywords "blog to book," and "blog-to-book-deal," I estimate that about six blogged books were released each month in 2011, which would make that year hotter for blog-to-book deals than 2009. Here are just a few blog-to-book titles published after the so-called cusp of the trend.

- Reggie Solomon's *I Garden: Urban Style* (based on his blog of the same name) was released by Betterway Books in December 2010.
- Neil Pasricha's *The Book of Awesome* (based on his blog *1,000 Awesome Things*) was published by Berkley Books in April 2010.
- Martha Alderson's *The Plot Whisperer* (based on her blog of the same name) was released by Adams Media in October 2011.
- Jill Smokler's *Confessions of a Scary Mommy* (based on her blog *Scary Mommy*) was released by Simon & Schuster in May 2012.
- Amanda H.L. Transue-Woolston's *The Declassified Adoptee Essays of an Adoption Activist* (based on her blog *The Lost Daughters*) was published in October 2013 by CQT Media and Publishing.
- Mallory Ortbert's *Texts from Jane Eyre: And Other Conversations with Your Favorite Literary Characters* (based on a series on her blog *The Toast*) was released by Henry Holt and Co. in November 2014.
- Benjamin Dewey's *The Tragedy Series: Secret Lobster Claws and Other Misfortunes* (based on his Tumblr *Tragedy Series*) was released by St. Martin's Griffin in March 2015.

Most of the writers who landed these contracts simply blogged their way to a deal; some of them blogged actual books. In both cases, they turned out copy that attracted the attention of both readers and publishers, and they did it one post at a time.

How can you, too, accomplish this feat? How can you become the next big blog-to-book success story? You can do so by writing and publishing a successful book—one that gets noticed by readers and publishers—in cyberspace. You can do so by not only writing your book using blog technology but by successfully promoting it on the Internet so you build an author's platform, a fan base or readership, large enough to impress any literary agent or acquisitions editor at a publishing house.

WHAT'S A BLOG ANYWAY?

Many writers know little about blogging or refuse to learn. When you purchased this book, you placed yourself among those aspiring authors ready and willing to embrace twenty-first-century publishing technology. Congratulations! By doing so, you took an important first step toward getting ahead of your competition and meeting your writing and publishing goals as well.

Even though you are considering blogging a book, I won't assume you know what a blog is. So let's start with a definition: A blog is an open-source blogging tool and a content-management system that runs on a hosting system.

The word *blog* is a contraction of *web log*, a shared online journal in which a person can post diary entries about her personal experiences or hobbies. At least, that's how blogs began. Once upon a time, people considered blogs places to share their streams of consciousness. Now blogs feature content targeted to particular audiences and focused on specific subjects. Bloggers pick a topic, often in a niche, about which to write.

Typically a blog is written and edited by an individual *blogger* (noun). *To blog* (verb) means to write or edit a shared online journal and to add *posts*, or published content, to the blog. Some bloggers hire ghostwriters or use *guest bloggers* (posts from experts or other bloggers). *Blog maintenance* entails publishing posts to the Internet using blog technology and updating the blogging program and its features. Some bloggers hire experts to design or maintain their blogs for them.

While bloggers may write about personal experiences, business, news, politics, hobbies, sports, health, opinions, or just about anything else, blogs are anything but personal in the sense that bloggers publish them in cyberspace for anyone and everyone to read. Writing a blog is about as public as you can get. You may choose to write about a personal topic, but you'll do it publicly on the Internet.

Many blogs offer commentary on a particular subject, cover various aspects of the news, or offer expert advice on a specific topic. Blogs often combine text with images, include audio and video, and provide links to other similar blogs, websites, and online resources. Readers can comment on posts, making blogs interactive.

A blog also constitutes a type of website. For writers who may not feel capable of managing a website, a blog provides an online presence manageable by even the least tech-savvy people. Therefore, you can call a blog a website solution for the technologically handicapped.

WHO CAN BLOG?

Anyone can blog or become a blogger (but not necessarily a *successful* blogger). No one and nothing stops you from opening a free (yes, free) account with a site like WordPress.com, www.Blogger.com, or www. Typepad.com, and beginning to blog.

If you want a self-hosted blog (more on this in chapter five), you may need some help, or, if you are technologically adept, you probably could manage it yourself. A self-hosted blog does cost a little bit of money, but not much; you'll need to pay for a domain name and a hosting account. I recommend a self-hosted blog for your blogged book; I'll explain why in chapter five.

WHO CAN BLOG A BOOK?

While it's true that anyone can become a blogger, not anyone can blog a book. To blog a whole book you must have the ability to write a book from start to finish. This entails conceptualizing a marketable book, organizing the complete book, and carrying out the concept from the first to the last page—in this case by composing short, targeted posts written on a regular basis—and publishing it on the Internet.

Anyone who can write and whose writing is worth reading can blog. (Actually lots of people who have scant writing ability and no writing worth reading have blogs, write and publish posts, and call themselves bloggers.) However, the same rules apply to blogging a book as to writing any other nonfiction or fiction book. After all, even though you create your book post by post in cyberspace, you are still writing a book.

- You must have a unique, salable idea with a big enough market to make it worth writing.
- You need to have enough information to fill a book (a minimum

of 25,000 to 30,000 words, which is an 80- to 100-page book). In most cases, you'll need to fill significantly more pages than that to satisfy a publisher.

- You need to be—or become—the expert on your topic. In some cases, you can gain expert status by blogging and blogging well—an added advantage of this endeavor. The more great content you provide over time, the higher likelihood you have of being perceived as an authority on your subject. (How do you think I became the expert on how to blog a book?)
- Your blogged book must offer value to readers.

If you and your subject matter meet all these criteria, you are ready and able to blog a book. If you don't, you can still blog. You just may not want to blog a book.

Some people who have blogged for a while with no intention of writing a book later decide they want to turn their blogs into books. The majority of blog-to-book success stories come from bloggers discovered by publishers because of their successful blogs; they then had to mine a year or several years of blog posts for the best ones to fit into a book. This is most often called *recycling* or *repurposing* your blog posts into a book. Author, book designer, and professional blogger Joel Friedlander, however, coined the term "booking a blog," which I prefer to use. It's the reverse process of blogging a book. When you book a blog, you don't plan to write a book via your blog but instead later recycle posts into a digital or printed book; when you blog a book, you preplan your book and your posts for the express purpose of producing a manuscript for a digital or printed book.

WHAT SUBJECTS CAN I BLOG OR BLOG A BOOK ABOUT?

According to www.WPVirtuoso.com, in 2013 there were approximately 152 million blogs on the Internet with more added every minute. In fact, at the time of the report, the site claimed that 172,800 blogs were being added to the Internet every day. That's about forty new blogs per minute, or 2,395 per hour.

As of August 2013, 22 percent, or 2,200,000, of the top ten million websites ran on WordPress.[1] That means that these websites were blogs or had accompanying blogs. The same year, WordPress.com reported having sixty-three million-plus websites.[2]

Here are some other statistics from 2013.[3]

- www.Tumblr.com had 101.7 million-plus blogs.
- www.LiveJournal.com reported having 62.6 million blogs.
- www.Weebly.com stated it had twelve million-plus blogs.
- www.Blogster.com had 582,754-plus blogs.

What's the point? Each one of those blogs represents a subject; you can blog about nearly anything.

But should you choose just any subject for your blogged book? No.

Technically a blogger can, indeed, choose any topic. No blogging police will pull your blog off the Internet if the subject you choose for your blogged book is stupid or boring, for example. Also, no written rule says, "You can blog books only on these particular topics." However, some blog subjects simply don't lend themselves to books.

Some blog subjects are too personal for a book, such as the blog my physical therapist started so he could share photos and news about his newborn baby. Some blogs aren't written in a style that lends itself to printed-book form. Of course, nothing stops you from blogging your book for your own enjoyment—market or no market, a subject too personal or not, or appropriate or inappropriate style. Readers will show up anyway. You can always invite your friends and family to read your blogged book. Without a marketable subject, however, you won't gain many unique visitors (readers) or subscribers, or page views, and you likely won't attract an agent or publisher.

Also, the market for some blog subjects is just too small. In other words, these topics won't generate enough readers to make blogging a book worthwhile. Typically, the larger the market for your book, the better.

That said, sometimes picking a subject that targets a specific small market can be a sound strategy. Big markets can be difficult to penetrate,

1. w3techs.com/technologies/overview/content_management/all

2. www.forbes.com/sites/jjcolao/2012/09/05/the-internets-mother-tongue and snitchim.com/how-many-blogs-are-there/ - sthash.IJ2KdZad.dpuf

3. snitchim.com/how-many-blogs-are-there/#sthash.IJ2KdZad.dpuf

especially if a lot of other bloggers or authors are doing a good job with them already. Niche markets can prove quite profitable.

I once wanted to write a book about the Jewish Sabbath. One publisher asked me to re-angle it to include all religions that celebrate the Sabbath, which would have given the book a larger market and made it more salable in that publisher's eyes. An agent, however, asked me to re-angle the topic so it narrowed that same book's market to only Jewish women. She felt the book would sell better—to a publisher and to readers—if the market was smaller and more focused. As you can see, one book idea can be written for any number of different markets.

Now you better understand why I said you can't blog a book on just any topic. In fact, if you want to blog a book, you must choose your topic as carefully as if you were planning to write a traditionally published or self-published book.

Just as they say "a rose is a rose is a rose," the same holds true for books, blogged or otherwise. A book is a book is a book.

CAN ANY BLOGGER BECOME A SUCCESSFUL AUTHOR?

If you want to blog a book, approach this endeavor like any other book project: Put aside your writer's hat and put on your businessperson's hat before you begin. This allows you to look at the big picture of both your blog and your blogged book just as you would if you were writing an e-book or a printed book. Only when you do this can you decide if your blogged book represents a viable business proposition.

In fact, when you write a book, you create a business. Whether you self-publish that book or a publisher publishes it for you, it becomes a source of income. You also have to promote the book, which means you must develop marketing and promotion plans and implement them. You may go out and speak on the book's topic and earn money doing so, thus becoming a professional speaker in addition to a writer. You also may decide to offer other services, such as coaching, teleseminars, or home-study courses that relate to your book. All these activities constitute aspects of your business as an author and the particular business center comprising your book.

For this reason, business-focused bloggers and aspiring authors spend time researching their online and physical markets and competition, creating online promotion plans, and developing a strategy for building a platform on the Internet and off—all prior to publishing their first post. To decide whether or not your idea is worthy of a blogged book, you need to ask yourself many questions, including:

- Is my topic unique?
- Does what I have to say add value to my readers?
- Is there a market for this blog or blogged book?
- Who are my readers?
- How is my blog or blogged book different from the competition?
- How will I position myself in the cybermarket or brick-and-mortar market?
- What will I include in my blogged book?
- How will I organize the blogged book (and, thereby, my blog)?

In chapters three and four, we'll delve deeper into the business side of blogging your book. In the meantime, ask yourself this question: Are you willing to approach your blogged book like a businessperson or merely like a writer or blogger?

If you answered, "Like a writer," maybe you should consider your blog as a daily writing practice instead of as a book project.

If you responded, "Like a blogger," maybe you should simply pick a topic about which you feel passionate and write a few times a week for the joy of covering your topic; don't worry about whether or not your posts come together in any type of logical sequence. At some point in the future you may decide to book your blog. You also could use your blog as an "author's blog" to promote yourself.

If you said, "As a businessperson," you've joined the ranks of the most successful bloggers and nonfiction writers. Congratulations! In this day and age, successful bloggers and nonfiction writers also must be savvy businesspeople.

Next I'll discuss the advantages of blogging a book. After all, if you are going to consider blogging a book rather than writing a book in a more traditional and private manner, or booking a blog, you want to fully understand the reasons to do so.

CHAPTER 2

WHY BLOG A BOOK?

Before I discuss the real "business" of blogging a book—deciding if you actually have a book to blog—let's take a closer look at the advantages of blogging a book rather than simply writing and publishing one the old-fashioned way. In the introduction, I told you why I blogged this book. Why should you follow my lead? I know of at least ten reasons why blogging a book makes good strategic sense no matter how you plan to publish.

Very simply, you have two publishing options. First, you can self-publish in some form. This could entail producing a print-on-demand (POD) version, printing copies in volume, producing an e-book, or even creating an audio book. Second, you can publish traditionally. This involves finding an agent who can approach midsized or large publishing houses for you, or approaching small publishing houses on your own. When you blog a book, you can choose either of these paths for the final production of your manuscript.

REASON 1: A BLOG ALLOWS YOU TO PUBLISH AS YOU WRITE

Each time you write a blog post and hit the "publish" button, you publish your work. You send it out to the World Wide Web for anyone and everyone to read. You become a publisher, or a self-publisher. You become an author as well as a blogger.

Therefore, blogging a book gives you the opportunity to actually publish your book as you write it rather than waiting until you complete your manuscript. You stop waiting for someone else to say you are a good enough writer to have your work published, and you simply publish it yourself in cyberspace.

For many aspiring authors, a blog represents their first byline. If you've never had your writing published before, you'll find your blog a thrilling first publishing experience—one in which you get to become the editor and publisher, and the entire cyberworld becomes your possible audience. You get to be in control of what you publish and when you publish it. Wow.

If you have tried for years to find a publisher for your work, you will discover great joy in the fact that when you "submit" (or publish) your blog posts, you won't receive a rejection letter in return. Instead of watching the mailbox—snail mail or e-mail—you can keep an eye on your blog statistics to see how many readers show up. Yes, readers! You also can watch for comments from your loyal fans. Yes, fans! These activities are lots more fun than opening rejection letters from editors and publishers.

Blogging a book does not mean you have to give up on traditional or self-publishing routes. In fact, you can send literary agents, acquisitions editors, and publishers to your blog to read your writing. You can submit book query letters and proposals as you blog your book. You can produce an e-book or a printed version of your book when you finish blogging your manuscript.

Some writers may not want to "give away" their whole book online. Maybe you worry that a publisher won't want to offer you a contract if you have no new information to offer in a printed version. Or maybe you think your blog readers won't purchase a printed version of your blog if they've already read every post in your blog. Possibly you're concerned that the continued availability of the information on your blog will deter people from actually purchasing a printed book with the same content.

If you feel this way, pick and choose how much of your book to blog, and reserve some of your information for a self-published or traditionally published version. That's fine—in fact, it's actually a good idea. I held back two chapters and the conclusion of this book and added more than 32,000 words to the first edition, more than doubling the book's original page count. (See chapter four for more information on how to plan your content so you hold back just enough information to entice readers and acquisitions editors at publishing companies.)

In the meantime, you can call yourself a published writer and a publisher. You also can call yourself a blogger. And your work will be available for the whole world to read.

Isn't that what all writers want—for their writing to be available for readers to read?

REASON 2: A BLOGGED BOOK GIVES YOU EXPOSURE AND BUILDS PLATFORM

Many writers enjoy spending solitary time in their "lonely garret" with only the company of a hot cup of coffee or tea, a computer (or a pad of paper and a pencil), and a pet curled up at their feet. In fact, that's what most writers like best.

To become a published author, however, you must come out of the garret and socialize. You have to talk with people and engage them in your work. You must get involved and interact with others. If you don't do this, you won't develop an audience for your work. You won't build a pre-existing base of readers in your target market—an author platform—for yourself and your books.

If *platform* represents new terminology to you, it's time to become familiar with this word ... very familiar, very quickly.

A sturdy author platform should consist of a combination of many elements, such as:

- expert status.
- numerous appearances on radio and Internet talk shows and television talk and news shows.
- frequent guest posts on others' blogs.
- a well-known presence in online forums and social networks.
- large numbers of followers on social networking sites.
- popular videos, podcasts, Hangouts on Air, or blogs.
- frequent interviews on others' podcasts, videos, Hangouts, or blogs.
- your own Internet, radio, or television show.

- many published articles or books in print and Internet publications.
- an extremely large mailing list.
- frequent talks and presentations given to small, medium, and large groups.
- a popular column on a well-trafficked site, like *The Huffington Post.*
- a popular blog.
- in-person, online, or home-study courses.

You don't need all of these platform elements to actually have an author platform. One of these elements, if large enough, can comprise a platform. The more elements you use to build your platform, however, the stronger and larger it becomes.

Most of the items on this list have little to do with writing. That's what makes blogging such a great platform-building option; it involves writing and lots of it.

Traditionally the best way to build a platform involved going out and speaking to audiences, but today you can speak to your audience online via a blog. In fact, you can speak to many more people every day through a popular blog than you ever could via public speaking. (If you want, you can even speak using videos and audio by uploading them easily to your blog.)

Imagine one thousand or more people reading your blog every day (a pretty awesome thought). That adds up to a lot of readers per month—enough to impress an agent or a publisher. If even 2 percent of those readers purchase a book you authored, that amounts to twenty books per day. That's 140 books per week, or over seven thousand books in one year. A small or midsized publisher would be happy with those sales numbers. According to Nielsen BookScan, a data provider for the book-publishing industry that compiles point-of-sale data for book sales, the average U.S. book sells fewer than 250 copies per year and fewer than three thousand copies over its lifetime. That's a pretty unimpressive number, as is 565, the number of copies sold per year by average e-book authors, according to the estimates of Mark Coker, founder of Smashwords.

The other platform elements listed above have their place and remain important if you want to become a traditionally published author or sell many self-published books. However, remember I said that one platform element, if large enough, could produce a sound author platform? A successful blog can do just that. If you write a great blog and manage to draw enough readers, this can prove impressive enough as a platform element in a book proposal to land you a literary agent or a publisher—with or without other elements. It's also enough to successfully launch a self-published book.

Let me explain why. New technology, including that which makes blogging a book so easy, hasn't helped the traditional publishing industry, which has floundered in recent years. In turn, this has made it harder for an aspiring author to get her foot in the door at publishing houses. Publishers have become more and more reticent to take a chance on an unknown quantity—a first-time author with no track record of book sales.

A recent analysis of U.S. ISBN data produced by Bowker, the global leader in bibliographic information management solutions and the official ISBN agency for the United States and its territories, revealed that the number of self-published titles in 2012 jumped to more than 391,000, up 59 percent over 2011 and 422 percent over 2007. E-books continue to gain on print, comprising 40 percent of the ISBNs that were self-published in 2012, up from just 11 percent in 2007.[1]

The 2013 annual BookStats report by the Association of American Publishers and the Book Industry Study Group showed that 457 million e-books were sold in 2012 in comparison to 557 million hardcover books. The study also reported that e-book sales grew 45 percent since 2011 and "now constitute 20 percent of the trade market," although e-book sales actually have leveled off. Indie publishers, writers who choose to self-publish, have ridden the wave of the e-book trend. Smashwords authors, for example, had nearly forty million free downloads of their books in 2013 at iBooks alone, according to Coker.

New technology—e-book readers and POD presses—made this possible.

These facts represent great news for indie authors who have chosen to produce POD books and e-books, but it's bad news for traditional publishers. Even though Bowker estimated that the amount of

---

1. www.bowker.com/en-US/aboutus/press_room/2013/pr_10092013.shtml

How to Blog a Book

ISBN numbers purchased by traditional publishers increased by 9.51 percent in 2012 over the previous year (indicating that title output has rebounded and is now seeing steady, if not large, growth), in general the number of people reading books has decreased. According to data presented in March 2013 by David Walter, research and development analyst for Nielsen BookScan, at the IfBookThen conference in Milan, Italy, book sales around the world are declining. In 2012, sales in the U.S. dropped 9.3 percent and fell by 3.4 percent in the U.K.

That means that while the total amount of books published per year continues to increase, fewer people are reading books. It's no wonder that publishing companies take fewer risks on new authors, put less money into promoting new books, and are more cautious about the manuscripts they acquire. They want whatever assurance they can possibly find that the books they choose to produce will sell. If an author has a platform, this provides some semblance of assurance.

Therefore, if you blog a book and develop a large blog readership, you become more attractive to a traditional publisher than a writer who has written a manuscript and has not yet gained a built-in audience. By writing a book on your blog, you build a track record—maybe not of book sales but of blogged-book readers. That gives a publisher some confidence in you and your book.

Of course, you and the other writer with no audience could choose to independently publish your books. If you did, which one of you will likely realize more success? You—the writer with the blogged book, of course. The prebuilt author platform ensures you have sales upon the release of your book.

I'm sure that's why Chronicle Books teams up with Tumblr for the Great Tumblr Book Search as well. Tumblr bloggers have platforms. Some Tumblr blogs turned into books include *F*ck! I'm in My Twenties* and *Dads Are the Original Hipsters*.

REASON 3: A BLOGGED BOOK GIVES YOU EXPERT STATUS

According to Technorati.com, one of the largest digital advertising platforms, 56 percent of all bloggers in 2010 said their blogs helped them or their companies establish positions as thought leaders within their industries. Additionally, 58 percent said they were better known in their industries because of their blogs.

No matter a person's actual credentials, a published book always helps establish expert status. Expert status constitutes one board in an author's platform. Publishers and readers purchase nonfiction books from authors they perceive as experts in their fields.

If blogging can help a person—any person—build expert status, imagine what blogging a book can do. It not only can help propel you into the ranks of "thought leader" in your industry but also into the ranks of published author.

Of course, you must know your topic and have great and well-researched information to offer your blog readers. If you don't, no one will read your blogged book (or blog) or perceive you as anything but a fraud. If you offer superb information in the form of a blogged book, however, little by little—post by post—you will achieve expert status.

That expert status will help you get noticed online and off by readers, agents, and publishers—and even clients and customers, if you like.

REASON 4: A BLOGGED BOOK GETS YOUR WRITING READ—AND READ QUICKLY

Why do writers write? Some might answer, "Because they must." I believe writers write because they want someone to read what they've written.

They write because they want to touch someone with their words. They write because they want to reach out through their work and make others cry, laugh, learn something, be transformed, feel inspired, or in some way relate to their own experiences. They write to take readers on a journey, transport them into another world, or show them a slice of life. They write to help people and to share what they know. They write to have impact in a meaningful way.

With a traditionally published book, you might wait a year and a half or two years (or longer) after signing a book contract for your book to be published. Then you must wait for readers to actually find your book and purchase it. Your book may appear only in online bookstores, like www.Amazon.com; getting it into a brick-and-mortar bookstore may or may not happen. Unless you promote your book well (publishers don't do much promoting these days), readership can remain low. Remember what I told you earlier? BookScan reports the average U.S. book sells less than 250 copies per year and less than three thousand copies over its lifetime, and average e-book authors sell about 565 copies of a digital title per year.

If you independently publish your book, you will not have to wait a year or two while it goes through production. Once you have a completed manuscript, a book design, and a cover, your POD book can arrive in your hands and in online bookstores in four to six weeks, sometimes less. An e-book can arrive in online stores in even less time. Without good promotional efforts, though, you'll still lack readers, which means buyers.

A great book worth reading, coupled with strong and continued promotion, draws readers. These elements increase the chances of your writing being read. Indeed, it is possible to sell well over 250 or 565 copies per year and to reach larger numbers than average over your book's lifetime.

A blogged book works differently from a printed or digital book in several ways. The more you write, and the more you promote that writing (on the Internet and elsewhere), the more readers you attract before the book is actually published. Just as with a printed or digital book, if you have a good idea that adds value to readers' lives or touches them emotionally, people will want to read your blogged book. Therefore, they will "purchase" it; they will subscribe to your blog or visit each day to read what you have posted. And they will keep reading.

You do not have to wait to publish, or release, your blogged book. When you decide you are ready, you can hit the "publish" button and release that first post—a bit like your first installment—into cyberspace. Voilà! Your book now can attract readers. Of course, the whole book does not become available immediately; you release it post by post, day by day, as you write your manuscript. In this manner, your book gets read much more quickly than it would with a traditionally published or self-published book. (More on how to publish your posts in chapter six.)

When you begin publishing posts, you might have no readers. This is not unlike having no buyers. Then you'll have one … two … three.

(You can track this with a blog's statistics program.) Before you know it, you'll have twenty readers a day, then fifty. That equals 350 readers in one week—more readers in one week than the average traditionally published author has in a year.

Why blog a book? Because your writing will get read—and it will get read more quickly than with other publishing methods.

REASON 5: A BLOGGED BOOK ALLOWS YOU TO TEST-MARKET YOUR BOOK

No better way exists to test-market a book than to blog it into existence. Every good businessperson knows the value of test-marketing a product before investing a ton of money into mass production and distribution. The same value exists in test-marketing a book, and a blogged book represents an extremely effective and cheap way to test-market a book idea.

My former agent once told me to write and then self-publish one of my book ideas as a test-marketing method. If it sold well, he said he'd take it on. You see, if I had good sales figures for the book, if I could prove the book would sell and had a market, then my agent would feel assured he could pitch it successfully to a major publishing house and land a publishing contract for me. Publishers want to know books have markets and readers who are waiting and ready to purchase it. Publishers want a sure bet, not a long shot, especially with a first-time author.

However, while getting traditionally published offers a writer superb clout, by the time you've gone to the time, trouble, and expense of self-publishing to test-market your book, you might not care about a traditional publishing deal any longer, especially if you've managed to achieve success with your self-published book.

What if your self-publishing test-market venture fails and you sell just twenty copies? Then you are out the time, effort, and money you put into your business experiment as well as your dream of traditional publishing.

Consider instead blogging your book as a test-marketing exercise. Simply put bits of your book out into cyberspace each day or several times a week for free (or almost for free). If readers are interested, and you have something worth reading, they will appear out of nowhere!

If they don't come, well, then your test marketing has succeeded in demonstrating that your idea does not have merit, needs to be tweaked, needs more promoting, or should be aimed at a different market. Or maybe your "product" should be thrown into the circular file.

A blog is free or cheap, and easy to erase. If this blogged book doesn't pan out the way you hoped, just delete it. You can start another blog tomorrow just as easily and cheaply. Go back to the drawing board, and try blogging a book on another topic.

Remember, though, you do have to give the blog some time and put in the promotional effort to get the word out. Know that—and do that—before you simply decide after a week or two that your test-marketing effort has proven your idea a failure. It may not be a failure—your promotional efforts might have failed or been insufficient.

Blogs take a while to catch on—even with good promotion. Give your blog at least six months to a year (with strong and consistent promotion) before you decide to hit the delete button. Bill Belew, a professional blogger (that means he makes money blogging), claims new bloggers must post three times a day at a minimum until they reach one thousand posts if they want to accrue "real" traffic to their blogs. The posts need only be about 300 words long to be cataloged by Google (note that the Google algorithms change periodically). At that point, their traffic—readership—skyrockets. (See his book, *How Wilby Got 20 Million People to Read His Blog and How You Can Too.*) Not only that, imagine how many words you would write in one thousand posts. That's 300,000 words or five books in about ten months!

Technorati used to index and rank blogs by something called "Authority," which involved standing and influence in the blogosphere. (You can find more on this topic in chapter seven.) According to the 2011 Technorati State of the Blogosphere report, the top one hundred bloggers, ranked by Authority, posted to their blogs more than six hundred times per month (which equates to more than twenty times per day). The Technorati top five hundred bloggers posted to their blogs more than 350 times per month (more than ten times per day), and the Technorati top five thousand bloggers posted to their blogs more than one hundred times per month (more than four times per day). That should give you an idea of what it takes to get your blog noticed in the blogosphere.

Gina Trapani posted to her blog, *Lifehacker*, twelve times a day every weekday for nine months. This got her an e-mail from an agent and a book deal for what became *Lifehacker: 88 Tech Tricks to Turbocharge Your Day* (Wiley 2006).

Not all people want to subscribe to a blog that sends them three or twelve posts a day. You need to know your readers, determine how fast you want to blog your book, and decide to what type of writing and posting schedule you can commit. I'm simply making the point that you do need to blog often and for a fairly long period of time—and promote that blog so people know it exists—before a decent number of readers shows up. In fact, it can take more than a year before you know if your blog has an audience. On the other hand, with really great promotion and lots of blog posts, you might know in a month or two if your market responds favorably. Plus, after six to twelve months, your book will be written, and you will be ready to self-publish it as an e-book even if you haven't garnered a ton of readers. There's hardly any cost in producing an e-book, and you might make a bit of money in sales, so your work will not be for naught. You also can self-publish a print book if you like.

Just like potential readers go to the bookstore or to Amazon to purchase a book, they search online for blogs to read. If they find your blogged book among the thousands—no, millions—of others and like it, they'll "buy" it, meaning they'll return more than once to read it or they'll subscribe to your RSS (really simple syndication) feed so it shows up in their browser each time you post. Maybe they'll even subscribe to it via e-mail, if you provide that option. They'll also tell their friends about it by sharing the link to your blogged book. (This is a bit like giving someone a copy of a book.)

If a lot of people do this, you'll know you have a winning book on your hands. If they don't, you'll know you need to go back to your research and development phase. Either way, you'll have successfully completed your test marketing.

REASON 6: A BLOGGED BOOK PROVIDES A DAILY WRITING COMMITMENT

Writers write. That's what we're told. However, often writers don't write.

To successfully blog a book, you must write regularly. Hopefully, the blog becomes a daily writing practice or commitment.

Once you begin blogging, to gain readers you must post frequently. The more often you post, the more quickly you'll gain readers. Remember what Bill Belew said: You need to write three posts a day until you reach one thousand posts. Or you can just post three times a week; that's enough, too. I posted one time a day on weekdays for eleven months on my blog *Write Nonfiction NOW* (WriteNonfictionNow.com). I then cut back to two days a week and now post Monday and Wednesday. On *How to Blog a Book* (HowToBlogABook.com), I wrote three or four times a week for five months, until I had finished the manuscript. Then I tapered off to Tuesday and Thursday.

The more often you write, the faster your readership will grow. The more content on your blog, the more likely the spiders, bots, crawlers, and such (the automated processes that search engines like Google and Yahoo use to index billions of Web pages) will discover your blog. When they do, your blog will get search-engine ranking, which makes it possible for readers to find it. Someone searching for your topic on Google, for instance, will discover your blogged book because your link comes up on a search page—hopefully at the top. Producing lots of keyword-rich content—content with words related to your topic that might be used in an Internet search—provides one of the best search-engine optimization (SEO) tools around. (More on this in chapter six.)

Blogging a book, rather than just blogging, means you provide a continuous flow of posts. Most blogs have random, unconnected posts. A blogged book must have posts that follow in a logical sequence, just like the content in any printed book. (However, each post must stand alone as well.) In fact, your readers will wait for the next installment. This provides even more incentive to you—the blogger—to write on a regular schedule. It also provides incentive for readers to return.

Consider employing deadlines that inspire you to write regularly. In addition to making a commitment to posting every day, every other day, or three to four times per week, you might want to post at a certain time or on certain days. Such commitments help ensure you actually do the work.

I blogged this book by writing three to five posts per week. I did not write them on a schedule. I had no deadline other than my quota of posts per week. I could, however, have required myself to post them on Monday, Wednesday, Friday, and sometimes Saturday at 10 A.M. Then my blog readers would have known when to expect a new post. (I didn't do this because I didn't want the stress of the added deadline. Plus, I had no problem writing the book regularly without that extra incentive.) As I already mentioned, I have another blog where my readers do expect me to publish a post on Monday, Wednesday, and Friday. I try to do so in the morning so the post gets the most exposure during the day in all time zones across the U.S., but sometimes I squeeze it in late in the day or evening. I rarely miss posting on that schedule, though.

With this sort of commitment, your book surely will get written. When I wrote the post that made up this section of this book, I already had completed 5,000 words by simply writing about 300 words per post over the course of about five weeks. That's not a lot of words per day. In fact, you could write more and post more often. You could post three times a day and write about 1,000 words per day. You'd complete your book fairly quickly and possibly gain readers much faster as well.

REASON 7: A BLOGGED BOOK ALLOWS YOU TO GET FEEDBACK ON YOUR WRITING

The fact that readers have the ability to comment on your book offers you, the blogger, one of the greatest reasons to blog a book. This aspect of blogging a book goes beyond test marketing and allows readers to give you feedback, ask questions, and dialogue with you about your product. Plus, you can engage in a conversation with your blog readers almost like you would in a focus group.

Many writers join critique groups so they can have other writers read or listen to their work and offer feedback. However, when you receive comments from your blog readers via the comment feature on your blog, you get to hear from the people who would purchase your book in a bookstore. This offers you invaluable feedback.

The comment function on a blog also gives you a chance to enter into a dialogue with your readers. When they choose to comment on what you have written, you can reply and ask readers questions or encourage them to continue conversing with you about the book, its content, your writing, and so on. Since these people represent your true readers, they offer the best feedback possible—even better than members of a critique group.

It's also possible to put surveys on your blog to ask your readers how they feel about what they read, if they are interested in reading about certain topics, or what aspects of the blog they find useful. This type of input from your readers can prove invaluable as well; you can implement the information you receive immediately by rewriting or editing posts, adding posts, or altering your writing strategy on future posts.

In addition, you can add a forum to your blog. This allows readers to become part of a community where you can interact with them and listen to their conversations. Inside the forum you can discover their interests and concerns and ask them questions, all of which provide fodder for your blogged book.

REASON 8: A BLOGGED BOOK ENSURES YOU COMPLETE YOUR MANUSCRIPT

Many writers start book projects and don't finish them. This is especially true for nonfiction writers who want to become traditionally published. Unlike fiction writers, who must submit a completed novel along with a brief proposal to an agent or acquisitions editor, nonfiction writers need only submit about twenty-five pages of a completed manuscript as part of their book proposal. If they then wait for a publishing deal, they may never finish their book. Instead, they may go on to work on another book proposal, starting the next book and never finishing that one either (if they fail to hook the interest of a publisher).

As part of a book proposal, a nonfiction writer needs a platform; without a platform the traditional publishing contract may never show up. Novelists can increase their chances of landing book deals by building an author platform as well. Since having a presence on the Internet represents one board in a platform, you might as well blog your book while you wait for an agent to pick you up or for an offer to come in from a publisher. Blogging your book prevents you from stopping your writing activity at page 25, 50, or even 100.

Believe me, I know the value of this. I've completed at least five or six book proposals, which means I also have about five or six unfinished nonfiction books.

You might argue that anyone can start a blog and then stop writing it at any time. You can even delete it. It would disappear from the Internet as fast as it showed up.

I can't disagree with this argument. Consider, however, your readers. What would they think if you suddenly stopped writing?

Here's my point: Once your blog has even a few regular readers, you are more inclined to keep blogging your book until you've completed the whole manuscript. Your readers and subscribers become your "accountability partners." You know they wait for you to post something. They want to "turn the page"; they want to finish reading the book, which means they want you to complete the manuscript. You can't let them down. You have to act responsibly and keep writing until you've posted the last word of your manuscript.

If you stop in the middle, you not only disappoint all your readers, but you also fail publicly. No one likes to do that.

I end up feeling guilty when I don't publish a blog post for a few days. (I have four blogs and two online columns.) I can't imagine how badly I would feel if I just stopped writing a book I was composing in real time in cyberspace if I knew people were reading it.

That's why I argue that no better way exists to ensure you finish your manuscript than to blog your book.

REASON 9: A BLOGGED BOOK SHOWS WHAT YOU'VE GOT … BUT NOT EVERYTHING

Many people ask me whether they should include everything in their blogged book. They are afraid to "give it all away." In fact, you don't need to give it all away if you don't want to do so.

It's true that if you blog every last word of your manuscript and publish it in cyberspace:

- a publisher might not want to offer you a contract for a printed book.
- some readers might not want to purchase your self-published book or e-book because you aren't offering new content.

You can get around these issues and still blog your book. For nonfiction authors, if you hold back some of your material, you can:

- attract a publisher with the fact that you still have plenty of new material to offer—and your blog readers already love what you've written and published.
- convince your loyal blog-book readers they should buy your self-published book or e-book because it contains more of the great information you provide on your blog.

Actually, agents and acquisitions editors prefer that you hold back a bit so they have new material to include in the printed version of your book—should you wind up with an actual publishing contract. Not showing all your posts, so to speak, can offer an advantage in the form of added value for a publisher. They don't want to reduce the value of what's available online, but they do want to add value to the printed book.

Should you decide to self-publish your blogged book, you might want to keep the same principle in mind. From this perspective, you could consider your blogged book a skeleton of the complete book. You might provide most, but not all, of the material and go back later to fill in the gaps. You can use it as a way to write full steam ahead without stopping to worry about the missing pieces, and then you can attend to those pieces when you get ready to write your second and more complete version.

For many writers, this approach feels much less stressful and overwhelming. Therefore blogging a book becomes an easier, faster, and more pleasant way to write the first draft of a book.

As I edited my blogged book, I found I added and changed a fair amount, and the word count more than doubled. Plus, as I mentioned,

I purposely left out two whole chapters from the blogged version and they became added features in the printed book.

Fiction writers can blog a successful novel and build their platforms to interest agents and publishers in the next book if they aren't interested in the blogged book. They will see your efforts as willingness to promote creatively and aggressively, making you a more attractive publishing partner—especially if the blogged book is a big hit.

REASON 10: A BLOGGED BOOK LETS YOU AND YOUR BOOK GET DISCOVERED!

Editors and acquisitions editors from publishing houses continue to troll the Internet in search of successful blogs as fodder for new printed books. One of those deals could have your name on it.

If you want your blog to get discovered:

- pick a topic about which you feel passionate.
- know you have enough material to keep you busy writing for a long time.
- be certain other people are interested in your topic.
- ensure you add something new and unique to the overcrowded blogosphere.
- write great content (content readers want, need, enjoy, or connect with emotionally) often and consistently.
- promote your blog and your posts well.
- don't give up.

If this list seems overwhelming to you right now, don't despair. You'll find all the information you need to accomplish these steps in the following chapters—with the exception of tenacity, which you must create for yourself. To help with that, I suggest you familiarize yourself with the stories of successful blog-to-book authors to keep you inspired. You can find interviews with nine of those authors in chapter eleven, but here's a rundown on just a few of the more well-known blog-to-book deals.

Julie Powell received a book contract for a memoir she wrote based on her blog *The Julie/Julia Project*. This book was then made into the

2009 hit movie *Julie & Julia*, written and directed by Nora Ephron. Powell blogged about cooking all 524 recipes in Julia Child's *Mastering the Art of French Cooking* during a single year. Ephron's screenplay is adapted from Powell's memoir and from *My Life in France*, Child's autobiography written with Alex Prud'homme.

Lizzie Skurnick received a publishing contract for a children's literature/young adult book from HarperCollins for her blog at Jezebel.com, *Fine Lines*. In this column, Skurnick analyzes classic young adult books, deconstructing them with wisdom, humor, and incredible insight. The book, *Shelf Discovery*, includes work that has appeared on the blog, as well as new work.

Emily Benet's book *Shop Girl Diaries*, a lighthearted comedy, began as a weekly blog about her experiences working in her parents' eccentric chandelier shop. It was picked up by Salt Publishing as a book and as a short film, which was shown at The London Short Film Festival.

Sex After Sixty was discovered by the e-book publisher 3ones as Mary L. Tabor wrote her memoir live for all of cyberspace to read. It is now available as an e-book and a print book called *(Re)Making Love: A Sex After Sixty Story* (Outer Banks Publishing Group).

Shreve Stockton's *Daily Coyote* blog, which contained photos of and commentary about the coyote pup she raised after its parents were shot, was published by Simon & Schuster and given the same name.

Ben Huh acquired *FAIL Blog* in January 2008 with his company, Pet Holdings. It contains a collection of humorous photos and videos depicting various kinds of failure. After being contacted by several agents, Huh sold the content to William Morrow Paperbacks, who turned the blog into *Fail Nation: A Visual Romp Through the World of Epic Fails*.

Pamela Slim started blogging as an assignment for a class about building platform and online business. Her blog, *Escape from Cubicle Nation*, shows readers how to bust free from their three gray walls and start their own businesses. She received a book deal from Portfolio Hardcover for *Escape from Cubicle Nation: From Corporate Prisoner to Thriving Entrepreneur*, a guidebook containing her best material.

Walker Lamond's blog offered fatherly advice on how to be a good man. He got a deal from St. Martin's for *Rules for My Unborn Son*, which, like the blog of the same name, offers a collection of advice from father to son.

Stuff White People Like, by Christian Lander, reportedly got a $350,000 advance from Random House Trade Paperbacks for this satirical look at the stereotypical behavior of white people. The book and the blog share the same name.

Postcards from Yo Momma, a blog by *The Observer*'s Doree Shafrir and Jezebel.com's Jessica Grose, includes entries about stupid e-mails written by mothers. The book version, *Love, Mom: Poignant, Goofy, Brilliant Messages from Home*, was contracted by Hyperion.

Here's my favorite: During the worst year of his life, Canadian Neil Pasricha decided to focus on the positive and come up with one thousand simple, free, awesome things most people take for granted, posting one each day on his blog, *1,000 Awesome Things*. Pasricha won two Webby awards, which are the Oscars of the Internet, and a book deal. *The Book of Awesome*, published by Amy Einhorn Books/Putnam contains two hundred of his awesome things.

Other bloggers who landed deals early in the blog-to-book trend include:

• Leo Babauta's *Organized Simplicity*
• Brett and Kate McKay's *The Art of Manliness*
• Joe Ponzio's *F Wall Street*
• Laurie Perry's (Crazy Aunt Purl) *Drunk, Divorced & Covered in Cat Hair*
• Grace Bonney's *Design Sponge*

Have I convinced you? Of course, these writers drove traffic to their websites. They wrote great content. They blogged often. Some of them even contacted agents. And they were discovered. More bloggers have done the same.

You can do what they did. In fact, you can do better than they did. You can do more than just blog—you can blog a book. And you can be discovered while you do so.

I've given you ten good reasons to blog a book. Now it's time to look at the nitty-gritty process of actually planning and blogging one.

CHAPTER 3

HOW TO PREPARE TO BLOG YOUR BOOK

As a blogger, you can simply begin blogging on any topic. However, if you want to attract a lot of readers so an agent or acquisitions editor "discovers" you and your blog or blogged book, you need to do some serious planning prior to publishing the first post. To ensure you build platform and get your blogged book noticed—by readers, agents, and acquisitions editors—prepare to blog your book before you write one word on that blank computer screen or post it on the Internet.

CHOOSE A TOPIC

To begin blogging a book, first choose a topic. While this step seems pretty obvious, there's more to it than meets the eye. You can choose any old topic and start writing, or you can choose a topic that attracts readers. I suggest you do the latter.

Optimally you would choose a topic that interests you *and* many others. In fact, it's best to choose a topic you feel passionate about since you'll be covering it for a long time. You don't want to choose a topic you'll dread blogging about each day. You want the writing to be both fun and interesting and your subject to motivate you to post.

Even better, find a topic about which you feel a sense of purpose—a mission. When you feel compelled to write about a topic because you are fulfilling a purpose, you also will feel passionate about that topic. When you combine your sense of purpose with your passion, you will feel inspired to write. This will come through in every post, in turn inspiring those who read your blogged book. If your topic also interests others—that is, it has a market—and is unique and necessary in its bookstore category, you've chosen a winner.

Knowing something about your topic helps if you write nonfiction, but you can research a subject as you write if you are not an expert. Your blogged book will have to contain expert information, though, so be certain the information is available. Many people who write books find it necessary to conduct lots of research to complete their manuscripts—even novelists. The same holds true for a blogged book. You can become the expert on your topic if you are willing to put in the time and effort.

If your topic meets four or five of the above criteria, your blogged book will achieve at least some degree of success. Here's a quiz to help you determine if your topic has a chance of becoming a successful blog or blogged book.

1. Does your topic interest you?
2. Does your topic interest a lot of people?
3. Do you feel passionate about your topic?
4. Do you feel you can write about this topic for a long time— several years?
5. Are you an expert on your topic?
6. If you aren't an expert on your topic, can you find information about it easily or access other experts to help you find information?
7. Do you have a sense of mission or purpose about your topic?

If you answered yes to questions 1 through 5, your topic may, indeed, be a winner. Affirmative answers to questions 6 and 7 increase that likelihood; however, these criteria are not necessary for success, just helpful.

At this point, you might want to check what other blogs exist on your topic by visiting blog directories, like www.Bloglovin.com or www.BlogCatalog.com. Or simply perform a search on Google by specifying your subject and the word *blog* in the search engine.

Then choose a unique angle for your blog. You want your blog to stand out from the crowd of other bloggers writing on your subject. The fact that you are blogging a book will set you apart to some extent—if you let your readers know you are doing so, since most other bloggers will simply be blogging on your topic, but you'll need a bit more of a hook than that. So consider what others are writing about and choose an angle that works for you and is different from what others have already chosen.

In the next chapter we will discuss in further depth how to analyze the competition in your subject area.

DECIDE WHY YOU WANT TO WRITE THIS BOOK

This may seem like a silly question, but why do you want to blog (or write) a book?

Think about it ... what do you want to achieve by blogging (or writing) this book? What's your purpose?

- Do you want to help others?
- Do you have knowledge you feel compelled to share?
- Do you feel you can change the world with your story?
- Is the timing just perfect for you to blog (write) this book?
- Have you been waiting for years for science to catch up with your theories? Did someone recently reveal new evidence to support what you've known all along?
- Do you have the solution to a problem and feel you must share it?
- Does a book offer you a way to gain customers for your business?
- Will a book prove you are an expert on your subject?
- Do you want to inspire people?
- Do you want to tell stories?

I mentioned earlier that a purpose or mission makes it easier to blog a book because you will be writing about your topic for a long time—probably long past the time when you finish blogging the actual book. It gives you the incentive to keep on writing. Additionally, if your book shares your sense of purpose, it gives readers an incentive to keep reading. That's why your blogged book must fulfill your purpose or mission: This gives it a reason to exist. If your blogged book doesn't have a purpose or mission, no one will show up to read your posts day after day.

The big question you must answer is: What's your mission? In other words, what do you want to accomplish by blogging this book? Do you have some driving reason to blog it now? Does doing so fulfill your purpose? What's in it for you? Wealth? Fame? Clients? Expert status? Satisfaction? A new business? Fulfillment? And what's in it for your readers? A solution? Much-needed help? A journey? An experience? Inspiration?

I must point out that if you are blogging a book for the express purpose of furthering your image, status, or business, your blog and book may not achieve the kind of success you desire. The purpose or mission I'm talking about goes deeper. At the risk of sounding New Agey and spiritual (and possibly turning some of you off), I'm going to suggest that you consider whether you have a mission that feels like your soul purpose. Maybe your mission relates to the reason you began doing the work you do. Did you feel called to become a doctor, lawyer, politician, parent, artist, writer, techie, accountant, or whatever you are? Why? What did you hope to accomplish? Who did you hope to help? What were your grand hopes and dreams? Therein lies the reason to blog your book—and the purpose or mission it must fulfill.

Why must you write this book? Be clear and precise about the answer. Write it down. Compose a mission statement: one paragraph that describes why you feel compelled to write or blog this book now.

CREATE A TITLE FOR YOUR BOOK

Your blogged book (or any book) needs a title, and possibly a subtitle, that entices readers into its posts and later its pages. Sometimes books have creative titles. Not everyone who blogs a book writes nonfiction, but nonfiction lends itself well to being blogged. Many nonfiction books have tell-it-like-it-is titles that let readers know exactly what they will gain by reading. Titles like this make it easier for readers to find your blogged book on the Internet because they are easily discovered when search terms are placed into a search engine. (Search terms are the words and phrases people type into the search forms of search engines like Google, Bing, Internet Explorer, or Yahoo.) If you are writing fiction, your title must tell readers what your book is about or what it is related to in some way; if it is a creative title, readers conducting Internet searches won't be able to find it easily.

To come up with a great title, first determine your book's subject and content. If you are having trouble coming up with a title, you might still be unclear about your topic or its angle. Skip ahead to the next two sections, "Hone Your Subject" and "How to Write a Pitch for Your Blogged Book," and complete them first. Then study how you have described your book. Look for phrases and words that might work in a title.

Often, titles use a play on words, alliteration, the actual name of the subject being written about, or a popular phrase. Sometimes titles evoke emotion. The title of a self-help and how-to book should identify or solve a problem, give a reader hope, be easy to remember, or be clear and specific to the topic.

Short titles are more memorable. Numbers work well, too, as in *7 Steps to …*, *10 Ways to …*, and *The 8 Places You Should … .*

Novel titles evoke a sense of person, place, time, and action. They compel readers to open the cover (or in this case visit the blog) by providing a hint of storyline, characterization, transformation, or theme.

The most important thing to remember with blogged books, though, is to use keywords or keyword phrases in your title and subtitle. These are the words or phrases on your website or blog that match popular search terms. They appear in the name of your blog, in its tagline, and in the titles, subtitles, and content of blog posts. Incorporating popular search terms into your title and subtitle makes it easier for the people seeking information to find your blogged book on the Internet. (More on this later.)

Here are some examples of blog titles and the corresponding book titles that resulted from their blog-to-book deals:

- **DAVID MCRANEY'S BLOG:** *You Are Not So Smart: A Celebration of Self-Delusion*
  BOOK TITLE: *You Are Not So Smart: Why You Have Too Many Friends on Facebook, Why Your Memory Is Mostly Fiction, and 46 Other Ways You're Deluding Yourself* (Gotham, October 2011)
- **LEO BABAUTA'S BLOG:** *Zen Habits*
  BOOK TITLE: *The Power of Less: The Fine Art of Limiting Yourself*

to the Essential ... in Business and in Life (Hyperion, December 2008)
- **LISA FAIN'S BLOG:** *Homesick Texan*
  BOOK TITLE: *The Homesick Texan Cookbook* (Hyperion, September 2011)
- **MATT GALLAGHER'S BLOG:** *Kaboom: A Soldier's War Journal* (formerly *Kerplunk: One Soldier's Journey from Baghdad to Brooklyn*)
  BOOK TITLE: *Kaboom: Embracing the Suck in a Savage Little War* (Da Capo Press, March 2010)
- **SHAUNA JAMES AHERN'S BLOG:** *Gluten-Free Girl*
  BOOK TITLE: *Gluten-Free Girl and the Chef: A Love Story with 100 Tempting Recipes* (Wiley, September 2010).
- **TUCKER MAX'S BLOG:** *Tucker Max*
  BOOK TITLE: *I Hope They Serve Beer in Hell* (Citadel, January 2006)
- **ZOE MCCARTHY'S BLOG:** *My Boyfriend Is a Twat*
  BOOK TITLE: *My Boyfriend Is a Twat: A Guide to Recognizing, Dealing, and Living with an Utter Twat* (Friday Project, August 2007)
- **LAURIE PERRY'S BLOG:** *Crazy Aunt Purl: The True-Life Diary of a Thirty-Something, Displaced Southerner Living in Los Angeles with a Herd Of Felines. Because Nothing Is Sexier Than a Divorced Woman with Three Cats*
  BOOK TITLE: *Crazy Aunt Purl's Drunk, Divorced & Covered in Cat Hair: The True-Life Misadventures of a 30-Something Who Learned to Knit After He Split* (HCI, October 2007)

I've mentioned a number of other blogs turned into books in the first two chapters of this book. Of course, my blog, *How to Blog a Book: How to Publish Your Manuscript on the Internet One Post at a Time* became *How to Blog a Book: Write, Publish, and Promote Your Work One Post at a Time.*

Notice that many blogs have fairly long taglines that serve as subtitles of sorts. These are often shortened or rewritten into a subtitle for the book. Mine is a good example, as is the one used by *Crazy Aunt Purl* (Laurie Perry).

Now it's your turn. Write a title and subtitle or tagline for your blogged book. Don't worry too much about it being set in stone. As you've seen, titles often change in the printed version.

HONE YOUR SUBJECT

While you might think you know what you're blogging about, it's always good to hone your subject. You can do that in a variety of ways, such as writing a synopsis or creating an outline of your book. However, when you distill your idea down to one, or possibly two, short sentences you easily can speak aloud, you truly know what your book is about. For this reason, I find writing a *pitch* offers the best method for fine-tuning your subject.

A pitch, also called an elevator speech—the one you might give to an agent or an acquisitions editor if you meet one in an elevator or at a conference—describes your blogged book in fifty words or less. (I usually tell my coaching clients to describe their books in twenty-five or fifty words.) Your blogged book's synopsis or outline might be a page or more in length. Try telling someone about the contents of your book by offering a synopsis quickly—in one minute—off the top of your head. It's difficult to do. However, giving someone your pitch—"pitching" them—is easy. Why? Because once you've written that pitch, you know the subject of your book. You've honed it to a fine point—just a few memorizable words. It's short and easy to remember. You'll recall it every time you sit down to write a blog post and every time someone asks you what you are blogging a book about. (If you'd like to learn more about pitches in general, you might want to read *Making the Perfect Pitch: How to Catch a Literary Agent's Eye* by Katharine Sands.)

If you do decide you want agent representation, you'll need a pitch. Most aspiring authors pitch an agent or an acquisitions editor at some point.

On the other hand, if you intend to self-publish, you may not plan on pitching your blogged book to agents or editors. Write a pitch anyway to polish your idea until it shines. Once you've written the pitch, your book naturally will flow from it, and you'll find that it becomes much easier to write your manuscript. That's the beauty of having composed a pitch—and as good a reason as any for going to the trouble of doing so.

After you've used your pitch to hone your subject, your pitch will continue to come in handy. It will serve as a quick and simple marketing or promotional tool for telling people what your blogged book is about—and convincing them to purchase it. You want to have the ability to tell someone quickly the gist of your book, including its benefits, unique qualities, and highlights.

Preparing to blog your book involves being clear about what you are blogging about, why you are blogging a book, and how you are going to move forward both with your writing and blogging. A pitch serves as the starting point for your writing and for all your promotion and marketing. Once you can tell someone in a short, pithy statement what your blogged book is about, everything falls into place. You know what your book is about, for whom you are writing, what benefit they will derive from your book, and what you must deliver in its pages.

HOW TO WRITE A PITCH FOR YOUR BLOGGED BOOK

To write your pitch, start by describing the subject of your blogged book in seventy-five words or less. Then edit this down to fifty words or less. Then see if you can edit it to about twenty-five words.

To come up with the content for your pitch, start by asking yourself, "What am I writing about?" This reiterates your subject or topic.

To determine your book's message, ask yourself, "What am I trying to say to my readers? What do I want readers to remember after they put down my book?" Or ask, "Why do I want readers to read my book?"

A pitch should include how your blogged book benefits readers. Try visualizing the back cover of the book. What type of copy might you print there? What message do you want to convey about what value lies within the pages of your book? (Even novels offer benefit to readers.)

Here are some things to think about and to include.

- Are you giving readers a solution to a problem? What is the problem? What is the solution?

- Are you answering your readers' questions? What are the questions? What are the answers?
- What does your reader want to know?
- What's your goal in writing the book?
- What do you want your readers to achieve from reading your book?
- Why is it important for them to read your book?
- What benefit will they get from reading your book?
- Is your reader in some sort of pain, and can you eliminate that pain?
- Can you make an emotional connection with your readers?
- Who are your readers? How many of them exist in the world?
- Is this book timely or time sensitive?

Include the title and subtitle, if you know it, in your pitch, but don't include them in the word count. Sometimes the subtitle actually can serve as part of the pitch.

Writing a pitch shouldn't be too difficult if you know what your book is about and why someone would want to read it. If you know what benefits your book will provide and how it will be unique, you should be able to write something short and pithy that describes your book perfectly.

Why the word limit? People have short attention spans. You have to grab them fast. You must learn to speak in sound bites. Plus, if you can't tell someone what your book is about in fifty words or less, then you don't know what you are writing about—and neither will they.

Try your hand at a pitch. Include your book's benefits, its unique qualities, why someone would want to read it, the problem you are going to solve, and the value it will add. What makes your book special? At its very core, what is it about? What is its message? What is its purpose? Fit all this information into the most creative twenty-five- to fifty-word sentence or two you can write.

Someone once told me if I couldn't write the subject of my book on the back of a business card, I didn't know what I was writing about. Can you do that? You may not be there yet, but if you go through this exercise, you'll be much closer.

MAP OUT THE CONTENT FOR YOUR BOOK

Finally, you need to know what content will go in your book. The best way to make this decision involves creating a "brain dump" of all the subjects you might cover. A brain dump gets all your ideas for your book onto paper so you can organize them. Think of it as uploading into one file all the data you've been storing in your personal computer that pertains to your subject. You also can conduct a massive brainstorming session on your topic to come up with all the ideas that could possibly become part of your book. Once you've finished, sort through the material and organize it into something that looks more like a book outline.

This exercise most commonly is called mind mapping. You can purchase mind-mapping software or download free software such as FreeMind. The easiest way to complete the exercise, though, involves purchasing a large poster board and some colored sticky notes. I like the rectangular kind with a paper surface on which you are able to write. You also can use colored pens or markers for this exercise, but then you can't move things around. Some people like to use a white board with erasable markers.

Put a large sticky note in the middle of the board and write your book topic on it. Now start writing related topics on the other sticky notes. If you are a very creative person but not very organized, just write down subjects on the sticky notes and stick them on the board. Don't worry about colors or where you put them. Once you have run out of topics, begin organizing them into related topic areas on the board by moving the sticky notes around. The new groupings become chapters. You can use a different-colored sticky note at the top of each grouping to indicate its general topic heading. As you group the sticky notes, you might get additional ideas. You can add these to the appropriate group or chapter.

You can color code as you go (if you are that organized). For example, for this book, I might use orange for all the topics related to getting started blogging a book, yellow for all the reasons you might want to blog a book, blue for all the blogs that have received publishing deals, and green for all the subjects related to how to write your blogged book.

Each subject grouping becomes a chapter in your blogged book. Each of the sticky notes in the groupings becomes a topic to cover in the chapter. Each topic may represent one post or several, depending on the depth it deserves or the amount of information you have on that topic. Remember, a blog post tends to be between 250 and 500 words in length. In your final manuscript, you might combine some of these under one subheading.

In chapter six, we will discuss how to write your posts and what to do with this rough book structure. For now, rest assured you have just created the basic content and tentative table of contents of your blogged book. Now you not only know what you are writing about, you also know how you will cover that topic from start to finish, from post to post. Get out a piece of paper or sit down at your computer and type out your table of contents. You also can make a list of all the different blog posts you will cover in each chapter.

If you had difficulty honing your topic by writing a pitch, try again after mind mapping your book. You can start over on a new pitch or revise the one you have already written. Getting a clear picture of your blogged book's content goes a long way toward helping you know what your book is about and fine-tuning your subject. You then can return to your mind map and search for gaps, redundancies, or other content issues.

RESEARCH VS. EXPERT SOURCE

While you don't need to be the expert on your subject to blog a book, by blogging about a subject and offering great information you become the expert. I'm a trained magazine journalist, and when I was in journalism school my professors taught me that a good journalist can write about anything by becoming the expert on the subject. A good blogger or writer can accomplish the same by becoming a good journalist and doing superb research for a nonfiction book or even for a novel.

However, that great information has to come from somewhere. At this point in the blog-a-book process, you must figure out what you need to know—if anything—to write your book. Look at the content you plan to generate, and ask yourself what research you need to do, what books you need to read, what experts you need to contact, and so on. Do whatever it takes to have all your resources ready at your fingertips before you begin writing so you don't have to stop to find necessary information. At the very least, know how and where to find these resources.

You may be able to fill in some gaps later, such as when you write your second draft for a publisher or edit your second draft for your self-published print or e-book version. In many cases, you will need the information immediately to actually write your first draft. You also may want to contact other experts for assistance.

It's possible that you *are* the expert on your topic. In this case, you may not require any other resources to get started.

Pause to evaluate whether you are the right person to take on this book project. Do you have the knowledge or the resources and access to experts who can help you compile the information necessary to write your book? Do you or will you be able to understand the information and disseminate it in an understandable manner for your readers? Can you carry out the project from start to finish given what you have just mapped out?

If you answered yes to these questions, and the steps in this chapter are clear, you are ready to move on to an essential endeavor: developing the business plan for your book.

CHAPTER 4

YOUR BOOK'S BUSINESS PLAN

Now you have to get serious. Really serious.

Anyone who wants to write a book—blogged or otherwise—needs to go through what I call the "Author Training Process." I used to call this "the book proposal process" because it entails compiling the information necessary for a book proposal, which serves as a business plan for a book. You don't have to write the proposal, but you do need to gather the figures, data, details, and particulars required for each part of a proposal, and you need to analyze this information. In my book *The Author Training Manual*, however, I explain how going through the process of producing a business plan for a book helps you become a successful author by training you to produce marketable books. That's why I changed the name of the process. Indeed, I thought the process was so important that I wrote an entire book about it.

As I write this, I can imagine some of you saying, "I don't need to write a book proposal." I know you might plan on simply having your blogged book discovered, and that's a good plan. Even if an agent or acquisitions editor finds you and your blogged book in cyberspace and offers you a traditional publishing contract, though, you will be asked to submit a book proposal. While an agent or acquisitions editor can read your blogged book online and decide if they like your subject matter and your writing, they still will want to know more about you and your plans for your blogged book. Therefore, you want to be ready to write a proposal (or have one already written), should you ever need one.

More important, it behooves anyone who wants to write a book, no matter how they plan on publishing it, to go through the Author Training Process. By doing so, you create a business plan for your book. You need to do that. Every book needs a business plan, and every aspiring or published author needs to function as a businessperson in addition to being a writer if he wants to succeed in the publishing world. So ask yourself if you really want to succeed with your blogged book. If you do, go through the Author Training Process.

The book proposal has served as the industry standard for creating a business plan for a book. That's why every traditional publisher requires one—and in large part adopts that proposal as its business plan once it signs a contract with a writer. Publishers also look at it as your business plan—and your commitment to them as their business partner—for your book. If you create the same document for your blogged book, you provide a sound business foundation for your book and make a commitment to follow through on the steps necessary for publishing success.

Don't make the mistake of viewing your blogged book as "just a blog." If you plan to blog a book, look at your blog as a manuscript in the making. Indeed, that's exactly what you are creating—a manuscript. Approach this endeavor just as you would any other new book project. It should be evaluated through the lens of an acquisitions editor, publisher, and sales and marketing team at a publishing house, all of whom would scrutinize the information in a book proposal before deciding to purchase and publish any new book idea. Every aspect—from content through promotion—should be planned out, and your business plan should prove your idea is marketable. As a blogger, you serve as the publisher of your book. Be a good businessperson and require a business plan for your book. Go through the Author Training Process, or proposal process, before you publish the first post.

FOUR REASONS TO LOOK AT YOUR BLOGGED-BOOK IDEA THROUGH THE LENS OF A BOOK PROPOSAL

If I haven't yet convinced you, let me give you four specific reasons to go through the proposal process. First, one day you may want to sell this book to a publisher, and you'll need a proposal to do so. I don't know of any traditional publisher that will take on a book project without first seeing a complete book proposal. Even novelists need some form of a proposal.

Second, a book proposal allows you to get a big-picture view of your book. As you compile the information necessary for your proposal, you'll look at your book through the critical lens of an acquisitions editor, evaluating its marketability and value-added potential both in cyberspace and on the bookshelf. You'll have to consider what makes your book unique in the market and how it will fare against the existing competition.

Third, since a book proposal includes a section on promotion, a proposal offers you a chance to think about all the ways in which you can promote your book, not just as a blogged book but eventually as a printed or digital book as well. In today's world of publishing, promotion is everything. A blogged book constitutes a great first step to developing a readership for your printed book or e-book, but you'll need to do more than just blog your book. You'll need to let people know your blog exists, and that takes promotion.

Fourth, a book proposal requires you to write an overview, a list of chapters (or table of contents), and a short synopsis of each chapter. These three sections provide you with a starting place for your blogged book (and for your book manuscript) and serve as a writing guide to follow as you blog your book into existence. They help you know exactly where your blogged book is going and what promises to keep to your readers along the way. Once you've completed these sections of your proposal, you're almost ready to begin writing your blogged book.

To begin blogging your book, you don't need a formal or complete proposal. You only need to go through the proposal *process*. Just compile the information necessary for a proposal. Do the required analysis. Hone your topic and content based on your evaluations, and create a promotion plan. After you've done these things, you'll have an extremely clear idea about what your blogged book will include, who will read it, how to make it stand out in the marketplace, and in what ways you will promote it. You'll also know if ways exist to build a business around your book with ancillary products or services. Perhaps even more important, you'll know who your readers are and what your competition looks like, if any exists. This information tells you if you should be blogging on this subject or not and how to do so successfully.

Completing the proposal process also tells you who else blogs or publishes on your topic. These people might make great joint-venture partners, or they could help by creating reciprocal links, providing guest blog posts, or promoting your book.

THE PARTS OF A PROPOSAL

Even though you won't actually write a book proposal to prepare to blog your book—although I encourage you to do so and be ready when an agent or acquisitions editor calls—it's important to know something about a book proposal if you plan to go through the Author Training Process. You can find many books on how to write a book proposal, and lots of information exists on the Internet as well. The following list includes the fourteen vital sections of a book proposal. Sometimes these sections are included in a different order; some books don't include them all. Authors and agents sometimes choose to include additional sections or even attachments. In my experience, most agents and publishers are happy with these.

1. Overview
2. Markets
3. Subsidiary Rights
4. Spin-Offs
5. Promotion
6. Competing Titles
7. Complementary Titles
8. Resources Needed to Complete the Book
9. About the Author

10. Author's Platform
11. Mission Statement
12. List of Chapters
13. Chapter Summaries
14. Sample Chapters

Since we are talking about blogging a book, if you don't plan to seek a traditional publisher for your book, and you don't want to go through the whole Author Training Process or create a complete business plan, you can do just the minimum. This means only planning out your manuscript and focusing on marketability. In this case, complete the following sections of a proposal prior to beginning to blog your book.

- Overview
- Markets
- Promotion
- Competing Titles
- Complementary Titles
- Outline
- List of Chapters
- Chapter Summaries

Completing this abbreviated proposal process provides you with a "big picture" of your book. When done, you will know who will read it, the markets to target with your promotion, what competition your blogged book faces, and what bloggers or authors to target for joint-venture projects. You also will have created a promotion plan to help you drive traffic to your blogged book and create platform. The outline you create will provide your book's structure: chapters and their content (blog posts). These proposal sections also give you a good overview of how to angle your blogged book so it holds a unique spot in both online and physical bookstores.

I highly recommend completing all the proposal sections. Better to be ready for the possibility of a traditional book deal if one arises. Plus, a business plan helps you meet your goal of successful authorship. If you complete the entire process, you have all the material you need, and you have evaluated your blogged (and printed) book for success. You will be ready for any opportunity, and you will have set yourself up for the highest likelihood of attracting both readers and publishers.

OVERVIEW: KNOW WHAT YOUR BOOK'S ABOUT AND WHY SOMEONE WOULD WANT TO READ (BUY) IT

The first section of a book proposal, the Overview, includes a lot of information in extremely condensed form because it provides a concise description of your book. If you write a proposal and submit it to an agent, this section has a hook (similar to a lead paragraph in an article); a pitch; an estimated number of pages, illustrations, etc., you plan to include in the printed book; and information on your book's features and benefits, as well as details on the back matter (glossary, appendix, resources). When you complete this section, you will know what your book is about and why someone would want to read (buy) it.

Writing the Overview for your blogged book helps you consider the full scope of your book's concept and its unique aspects and value. You see your book in totality. Also, just as the first chapter to a book entices a reader to continue reading, the Overview of a book proposal entices an agent or acquisitions editor to read the rest of the document and to consider publishing the book.

Once written, your Overview serves a variety of marketing purposes. You could use all or part of it in an "About" or an "About This Book" page on your blog, in promotional material featured in other places or documents (on your website or in material sent to prospective reviewers or people you would like to provide cover blurbs or testimonials), or even as your first blog post in which you describe what your blogged book is about. The first few paragraphs of the Overview might become the initial paragraphs of the first chapter of your printed book, as did a revised version for this book.

In the last chapter, you did some of the work necessary to write your blogged book's Overview. You came up with a title and honed your subject into a pitch. You also mapped out your content. You now should have a clear idea about how you will focus your blogged book, what types of topics you might include, and how you can make it unique. This is great fodder for your Overview. You will discover more about these issues, and possibly change the focus and angle, when you look at the Markets and Competing Titles sections of a proposal. For now, the information you have gathered will suffice.

Typically, an Overview begins with a few sentences or a paragraph or two that grab the reader. As mentioned, this isn't much different from a magazine article; the beginning of the Overview could be considered your "lead." Write something compelling. This could become the first paragraph or two of your blogged book if it is really enticing. For example, here are the first two paragraphs—the lead—to my *How to Blog a Book* proposal.

> For the last five years acquisitions editors have scanned the Internet to find new writers with great ideas that can be turned into books. Based on research done by Publishers Marketplace, experts estimate more than sixty blogs landed book deals in 2009. The database includes only announced deals; the total number was much higher.
>
> Some of the writers who landed contracts simply blogged their way to a deal; some of them blogged actual books. In both cases, they turned out copy that attracted readers' and publishers' attention, and they did it one post at a time on the Internet.

You'll find a semblance of these two paragraphs at the beginning of chapter one of this book. When I revised the manuscript, they changed it a bit, and then my developmental editor and line editor asked for more changes. In both forms they provide the necessary hook to interest someone—readers or an agent or acquisitions editor—enough to read further.

Next, insert your pitch—twenty-five to fifty words that describe your book (see chapter three)—followed by a statement that includes how many pages your book will have and how much back matter it will include. If you need a sentence to transition into your pitch, that's fine. Here's the paragraph in my proposal that followed the copy above.

> How can other writers accomplish this feat? The host of aspiring authors hoping their online writing efforts will get them discovered can find the answer to this question in *How to Blog a Book, A Step-by-Step Guide to Writing and Publishing Manuscripts on*

the Internet One Post at a Time. How to Blog a Book will be the first book to explain the basics of how to write and publish a successful nonfiction book—one that gets noticed by readers and publishers—in cyberspace. The finished manuscript will contain approximately 33,500 words, or 134 pages, and will have one page of back matter consisting of a bibliography.

Since your blogged book's form is a series of posts rather than pages, think of your manuscript pages as posts. How many posts will you write? Each post will be 300 to 500 words in length. A short book has about 25,000 words, which translates into about one hundred published book pages. Most publishers want at least 45,000 words (I was asked to add 10,000 words and an index to the first edition of this book), which pushed the printed book closer to two hundred published pages. If you assume the average post will be 350 words in length, you will have to write about 72 to 129 blog posts. Your back matter might consist of some extra blog pages with resources or appendices.

If you want to know the page count of your finished manuscript, convert the posts to manuscript pages by doing the math. Come up with an average number of words you will write per post, and multiply this by the estimated number of posts; then divide this by 250 words per manuscript page. This will give you the number of manuscript pages you will have when finished.

Now write about a page and a half that describes the benefits of your book. To do so, answer these questions: What will my readers gain by reading my blogged book? Once they finish reading the book, what will they have learned? Why should they read my blog or book? You can even list these as bulleted points. For example:

My readers will:

- gain an understanding of …
- learn how to …
- find out how to …
- discover the answer to …
- get tips for …
- change their …
- experience …
- be given the solution to …

The answers to these questions will provide the value-added aspect of your book and the last information necessary for the Overview.

Also, if your blogged book will contain any special features, such as sidebars in each post with tips, a special post once a month offering a meditation, a workbook element (questions to answer), or funny cartoons, mention them. Include information on how these features make your blogged book unique and add value to readers.

When completed, the Overview should read like a pithy marketing-oriented book synopsis condensed to about two pages. Consider this your promise to your readers and your enticement to potential book buyers and blog readers.

As you later blog your book, refer to the Overview to make sure you deliver on your promises and stick closely to your vision of the book. In this way, the Overview becomes a writing reference—another reason to write one. Combine the Overview with your table of contents and chapter-by-chapter synopsis (which I will discuss shortly) as you write, and you have a strong writing guide for a marketable book. This guide is better than any outline and will keep you on track as you blog your book.

MARKETS: ANALYZE HOW MANY PEOPLE REALLY MIGHT READ YOUR BLOGGED BOOK

With the first step in the proposal process completed, it's time to move on to the next section: Markets. Make sure you are wearing your businessperson's hat—no writer's hats allowed.

It's time to meet your readers and to discover how many readers your blog potentially could gain. In general, this represents an exercise in researching whether your blog or blogged book, or your digital or printed book, has a market. Is there anyone out there who will read it? Does anyone out there need your book?

Even though you are blogging a book, you need to know this information for two reasons: First, since you will be primarily responsible for promoting your blog, you'll want to discover where to place your promotional efforts. In other words, you want to promote to the right readers or in the right markets. Thus, you must take time to identify those readers. Second, and more important, you must find out if you even have potential readers. If no market exists for your blog, you'll be lucky to garner even a few readers for your blogged book. (If this is the case, forget about your blogged book getting discovered and made into a traditionally published book.)

If a market exists for your blogged book, you have a reason to write and publish your work on the Internet (or in physical form). To find out, answer the question "Who would read (buy) my book?" and then "How many of those people exist in my country or in the world?" Since you are blogging a book, you want to ask, "Is there anyone out there in cyberspace who will subscribe to my blog or come back every few days to see if I've published a new post—a new installment to my book?" In blogging or website terms, you want to know if you have a large enough market to attract a substantial number of unique visitors who will view many pages when they read your blogged book. However, if you also want to traditionally publish your blogged book one day, you should be concerned about the market for a printed book on your topic as well.

To discover if your book has a market, start with this step: Describe the audience for your blogged book. Who is your average blog reader? Who would be interested in your topic? Who will subscribe to your blog? Include demographic information if you can. Do your research!

Good places to do this type of research include:

- clubs or organizations related to your subject. Attend some meetings and see what types of people are members.
- online forums related to your topic. Join these forums and participate in the discussion; ask questions to find out what types of people are members and where else they hang out online. Then check out these places as well, and try to gain information on the people there.
- online groups related to your topic, such as those on Facebook or LinkedIn. Again, participate in the groups. Get to know the participants and members.
- bookstores. Check out what types of people are buying books on your topic.

- Google, Yahoo, Bing, and other search engines. Start poking around. Behave like a journalist and see what you can discover about the types of people who get involved in all things related to your topic.
- social networks. Ask questions of your followers. They'll enjoy responding.

Now describe large groups of people—actual markets—that will subscribe to your blog. For instance, if your blogged book will appeal to women, this market is huge and would be described this way: "According to the 2012 U.S. census, women make up 50.8 percent of the population. As of midnight 2014, there were 16,118,734 women in the U.S."

If your blogged book targets chiropractors, for instance, you might describe your market in this fashion: "Based on information from the American Chiropractic Association, more than sixty thousand doctors of chiropractic practice in the United States."

If your blogged book will be directed at the international Muslim market—an enormous one—you might write: "Muslims will comprise more than one quarter of the Earth's population by the year 2030, according to a study released in January 2011 by the Pew Forum on Religion and Public Life."

Again, do your research! Use a search engine and find statistics and information on the size of these groups. Check:

- www.Wikipedia.org.
- the U.S. Census Bureau.
- organizations that monitor or report on professionals in your subject area or the profession itself.
- organizations that regulate an industry related to your topic.
- major newspapers and publications, such as *The New York Times*.
- market research companies.

Don't be lazy. Answer the question "Who is the market for my blog about cats?" for example. Wrong answer: "People like me," or "People who like cats." Right answer: "Thirty-three percent of U.S. homeowners." Even better: "The 33 percent of homeowners who want to own cats." Use your favorite search engine and ask the right questions; you will get answers. Ask, for instance, "How many people in the United States own cats?" When I put this query into the Google search engine, I easily discovered that the Humane Society of the United States reported that 95.6 million cats are owned by residents of the U.S. as of August 2012. Even better, angle your blog to people who own cats with kidney disease. Then ask, "How many people own cats with kidney disease?" I couldn't find a statistic for the total number of cats in the U.S. with kidney disease, but a call to a vet informed me it is one of the most common ailments in cats, especially older ones.

Once you've done your research, you will know if your blogged book has a market or not. If you have large numbers of people who potentially could be interested in your blog, great! Your blog gets the green light.

SUBSIDIARY RIGHTS AND SPIN-OFFS: DISCOVER WAYS TO BRAND YOURSELF AND EARN MORE MONEY

If you are writing a complete proposal, the next section to tackle is Subsidiary Rights. When you sell your book to a publishing house, the publisher acquires primary book rights. As Michael Larsen explains in *How to Write a Book Proposal*, primary rights include publishing the book as a hardcover, trade paperback, and/or mass-market paperback; book club rights; selling permission to excerpt part of a book within another work; second-serial rights to excerpt the book, condense it, or serialize the whole book in a periodical after publication; reproducing the text in other forms and media; reproducing the text in a large-type or a royalty-free Braille edition; selling school editions; photocopying rights to all or part of the book for internal use by a school or business; selling the book through direct-response marketing channels; selling the book as a premium to businesses or nonprofits as a promotional tool; selling the book in bulk to customers outside the book industry; and granting the right to use part of the text to promote the book.

Subsidiary rights include things like television and feature film rights; foreign rights; first- and second-serial rights to excerpt the book before publication; translation rights; rights to produce abridged, unabridged, and dramatized audio and video versions of your book; merchandising rights; and software rights (including phone applications or apps).

Subsidiary rights can be seen as additional markets in some cases. This section also offers you a chance to think about how to build a business around your blog with different formats, products, and services, and to brand yourself with all of these.

While you are wearing your business hat—which you should still have on—consider whether your book has potential for subsidiary rights. While this section is not necessary to the blog-a-book process, and in many cases is left out of the initial book proposal written by the author (and added later by agents), I've included it here so you'll be aware of it. If you want to earn a living as an author, it's an important section to consider.

The Spin-Offs section constitutes a more pertinent section of a book proposal but also is not necessary prior to beginning to blog your book. That said, acquisitions editors and agents like to know you are more than a one-book author. It's also a chance for you to plan your writing career. The Spin-Offs section of a proposal asks you to think about what other books you might write as follow-ups to your first book idea.

Ask yourself: Could my book be a series? Does my book naturally lead me to write books on similar or related topics and create a brand for myself? Is there a way for me to entice a publisher into a multi-book deal?

If you want to be found by an agent or acquisitions editor, or if you plan on approaching a publisher yourself, it's a good idea to prepare yourself to answer the question "What other books do I plan to write after this one?" Your answer could make the difference between getting a contract and being turned down.

Additionally, this is a good time to consider what you will do when you finish your blogged book. How will you capitalize on that success? Having your next book idea lined up and ready to go means you don't lose your readers' attention. That's key to becoming a successful author over the long term. This type of planning can prove essential if you want to build a business of any type around your blogged book.

PROMOTION: DETERMINE HOW YOU WILL HELP SELL YOUR BOOK

For a blogged book, promotion primarily means asking the following question: "How are you going to let the cyberworld know your blog exists?" In other words, how will you "sell" your blog and your book?

It's time to add your social hat to your business and writing hats. To gain readers, you must promote yourself and your blog via social networking. Otherwise no one will know you've created a blog or begun blogging a book. While promotion can involve many activities, including speaking, advertising, search engine optimization, radio and television appearances, and video or audio podcasting, as well as social networking, the overriding thrust revolves around increasing public awareness of your blogged book and you as a blogger. To accomplish this, you must put yourself in the public eye. That's why I consider promotion a social activity requiring a social hat. Put it on, and get ready to use social networking, because it's one of the best tools for publicizing, or promoting, your blog.

As you complete the Promotion section of your business plan, don't forget that you need to promote your blogged book off-line as well as online. Why? One day it will become a printed book, and you need a plan now to gain readers for all of your book's forms: blogged, printed, and digital. Therefore, create a promotion plan that encompasses more than just the Internet. That said, the Internet is the place to begin your promotional efforts, especially given that you are blogging a book.

Promoting in cyberspace does not mean simply gaining friends on Facebook and followers on Twitter. It also means participating in forums and commenting on related blogs and online columns. It means joining LinkedIn and interacting with the groups on that site. It means getting involved in whatever is new, like Google+ and Pinterest were a few years ago, and posting to www.Reddit.com, as well as forming networks of bloggers who will help you get your blogged book noticed with reciprocal linking and agreements to submit each other's posts to sites like www.StumbleUpon.com. And you want to let all your social networks know every time you post a blog. That means including the link along with a short note in a status update.

You also can do more traditional types of promotion. You can:

- send press releases to the media.
- publish articles on your book's topic.
- set up speaking engagements, workshops, and teleseminars.
- send out a newsletter.
- use e-zine article-marketing techniques.
- make radio and television appearances.
- start a television show of your own.

Plus, you can (and should) create an expanded website that hosts your blogged book. That site might offer features that attract visitors and readers, such as articles, surveys, resources, and links to other blogs or your radio or television show. It can also have a media kit or author's page to help you get media attention and speaking engagements.

When it comes to promotion, think and act outside the box. Create contests, giveaways, and gimmicks to attract attention to your blogged book, your website, and yourself. Hire a publicist to help you with this task. And get involved in "untraditional" types of promotion that have become mainstream, such as podcasting, Google Hangouts on Air, video blogging (vlogging), and Internet radio shows.

You also can hire a search engine optimization (SEO) specialist. These experts can make your blog or website easier to find, whether blogged-book readers or ordinary individuals are doing the searching. They also may be able to advise you about online advertising options.

All of this falls under the heading of promotion, but most writers don't want to do this work. Their eyes glaze over, and they simply refuse. "I only want to write," they say. However, if you want your blogged book to be read, which in this case means found on the Internet, you must promote it. Period. If you want it one day to be read in book form—in other words, purchased—you have to promote it in the "real" world. Period. There is no way around this fact.

You have to promote your blogged book both because you simply want people to read it and also because you want an acquisitions editor to find it. You must have readers (and a good many at that) for an acquisitions editor to find your blogged book and feel it deserves to be published. You need to have gained large numbers of friends, followers, "tweeple," and connections in your social networks. You need a large number of unique visitors who seek out your blog. You also want your blog to have a sizeable subscriber and e-mail list. All of these figures go into a written proposal as part of your Platform section but come into play in the Promotion section as well.

Consider speaking publicly on the topic of your blogged book, making radio and television appearances, doing workshops and tele-seminars, writing a newsletter, going on a speaking tour, or anything else you can think of to promote your book. Include all of these activities in your promotion plan.

The Promotion section can make or break a formal book proposal. Publishing houses rely on you to come up with a great promotion plan, because it eventually becomes *their* promotion plan. A publisher adds to your plan but primarily relies on you to promote your own book in your own way. Most publishing houses do little these days to help promote new titles, especially those from first-time authors.

If you self-publish your book, your promotion plan becomes your business plan. This is your strategy for selling books. When you turn your blogged book into a printed book or an e-book, all those readers, friends, tweeple, connections, listeners, and followers hopefully run out and purchase it.

COMPETING AND COMPLEMENTARY TITLES: COMPARE THE COMPETITION AND DISCOVER IF YOUR IDEA IS UNIQUE AND NECESSARY

Now we come to the Competing Titles section of a book proposal. In the case of a blogged book and the proposal process, don't focus solely on books, though. Also study other blogs that might compete with your blogged book. This helps ensure that you are the only one blogging on your topic or that you are the only one blogging on that topic from a particular angle. You want your blog to be different from other blogs *and* books.

Put your business hat back on. You may, however, need to add in some creativity, so have your writer's hat handy. (No more need for your social hat at this point; you can put it away.)

If lots of bloggers have chosen to write about your blogged book's topic, don't be put off; that probably means readers find the subject interesting. If publishers keep publishing books on a certain topic, it means they think a market exists for those books.

On the other hand, you may find no one else blogging on your topic. That might prove a good thing—if a lot of people possess an interest in reading about it. You can make a name for yourself as the first and only one in that particular market. For example, I began blogging from a mother's perspective about boys in the dance world. My mission was to mentor boys and help parents of boys who wanted to become professional dancers. No one else was writing about dance and boys in dance from this perspective. I gained a loyal readership pretty quickly at *My Son Can Dance* (MySonCanDance.net). Additionally, when I began blogging a book about how to blog a book, no one else was doing this. I made a name and a place for myself in cyberspace on this topic (which later became attractive to a publisher).

If you find no other blogs on your topic, also consider that this might be for good reason: No one may be interested in your topic. It's possible, though, that no blogs exist on the topic because no one has yet thought about writing about your topic. If so, that's great! The market is just waiting for you. Buy a domain name that relates to your topic, set up your blog, and start writing and publishing fast! (More on how to do this in chapter five.) Then watch readers show up.

It behooves you to look not only at the other blogs that focus on your topic but also at what books have been written on it. Make sure the book you are writing is different and adds something new to existing titles on bookstore shelves as well.

The exercise of looking for competing blogs relates to two sections of a book proposal: Competing *and* Complementary Titles. So look at complementary titles, too. Complementary books are the related titles that readers of your book might purchase as well; these books do not represent competition per se. If there are many books on one complementary topic, you might want to see if your book fits nicely with, or parallels, these books, since obviously a readership exists for them. For example, Michael Larsen's *How to Write a Book Proposal* complements my book, *The Author Training Manual*. His book is only about how to write a book proposal to land a traditional publishing deal. My book discusses how to create a business plan for any type of book—indie or traditional—so you write a book that sells successfully; that plan is based upon a book proposal.

Don't forget to look at complementary blogs. These might provide opportunities for developing reciprocal links, guest posts, or joint ventures. The readers of a complementary blog might be just as likely to read your blog—or to purchase your books, products, or services at a later date.

It's easy to find information on competing and complementary blogs. Simply go to a blog catalog, like www.BlogCatalog.com, which offers listings of millions of blogs, or www.Blogorama.com. Sometimes you can find a blog network related to a certain subject area. Try doing a Google search for Web or blog rings, blog networks, or blog directories on your topic. My blog, MySonCanDance.net, is listed at www.DanceBloggers.com. If your blogged book involved a subject related to dance, you'd want to explore the blogs listed there, for example.

Look at the ranking of the blogs you find in a catalog, if it offers ranking, or the reviews. Examine the highest-ranked blogs as well as those lower down in the rankings.

Take all the information you gain from your research and compare your blogged-book idea to both the competing and complementary blogs and printed books. Ask yourself these questions.

- Does it still hold up? Is it unique?
- Does it need to be re-angled?
- Am I providing new benefits and features to blog readers who enjoy this subject?
- Do I need to rethink the content to make it stand out from the pack of other blogs or books?
- Will I choose to compete with the top-ranked published blogs or the ones ranked fifth, sixth, or even tenth? (You might find those lower down the scale an easier niche to break into.)

Be honest with yourself. This is your last chance to rethink, re-angle, and refocus your book's subject (and content) if you find your book is off base or has competition that is too similar. If necessary, make the changes to your idea now—before you start blogging—to ensure it truly fills a "hole" in the blogosphere and on the shelf of brick-and-mortar bookstores. Go back and redo your mind map and create a new pitch, overview, table of contents, and chapter-by-chapter synopsis if necessary. You also might need to rethink your markets. Taking these steps at this point ensures your success in both the cyber and the traditional publishing marketplace.

Reggie Solomon did a great job of finding a niche in the blogosphere with both his blogs, *Tomato Casual* (www.TomatoCasual.com) and *Urban Garden Casual* (UrbanGardenCasual.com). He looked at what already existed in cyberspace and found a way to provide something a bit different: a casual approach to everything under the sun for tomato lovers and to urban gardening.

RESOURCES NEEDED TO COMPLETE THIS BOOK: ARE YOU READY AND ABLE TO WRITE, PUBLISH, AND PROMOTE?

As you get closer to beginning to blog your book, consider this question: What resources do you need to complete your book? The answer to this question completes the section of a book proposal called Resources Needed to Complete the Book.

This section may not seem to pertain to many blogged books, and it is sometimes left out of an initial book proposal and added by the agent, but I suggest you include the research for it as part of the proposal process. You, the blogger, may find you need little besides your mind, your fingers, a computer, and an Internet connection to write your book. Well, every blogger needs a little bit of money to pay for an Internet connection and a website (since it's likely that you will eventually pay for a self-hosted blog—more on this in chapter five). You also need a computer.

Primarily this section does, indeed, cover costs. Here are the types of costs you might want to consider at this point in the process.

- **PHOTOS:** You might want to purchase a subscription to a stock photo provider, for example, or you might need a photographer for special needs.
- **ART:** You might need a logo or a series of cartoons to illustrate

your book, or you might want to purchase a subscription to an online clip art service.

- **PERMISSIONS:** If you reproduce large sections of an existing book, you must purchase the rights from the publisher.
- **HOSTING:** If you don't already have a website, you will need one. (Or you can opt for a free hosted blog.)
- **WEBSITE DESIGN:** If you don't already have a website and you don't know how to create one, you may need to hire someone to create a website for you. You can use your hosted or self-hosted blog as your website; however, even a self-hosted WordPress.org website may require that you hire someone to create an original design for your site.
- **INTERNET CONNECTION:** This is the monthly charge for your Internet service.

If you decide to self-publish your book, also include the cost of editing, designing (cover and interior), proofreading, indexing, and promoting your book.

In this section of a book proposal an aspiring author also declares how long it will take her to complete her book. After all, time is a resource. So take a moment—or a few—to set some deadlines. How much will you write each day, week, or month, and when will you "turn in" your finished book? In other words, how many blog posts will you commit to writing each week, and how many will it take you to complete your book? Given those figures, when will you finish your blogged book? Write that down. Make that part of your business plan for your blogged book.

ABOUT THE AUTHOR: WEIGH WHETHER YOU ARE THE BEST PERSON TO WRITE THIS BOOK

Are you the type of writer who feels certain you possess the expertise to write your book, or are you the type of writer who questions whether you are good enough to do so? Do you know you are the best person to author the book you have in mind, or do you wonder if someone better exists?

Either way, at this point you must write down all the reasons why you, indeed, are the best person to write your blogged book. In a nonfiction book proposal, this section is called About the Author. Sounds pretty simple, right?

It can prove to be simple—or hard. That depends upon you. To complete this exercise, write in the third person a biography of your expertise and experience. Include the most important facts first, such as anything that makes you the expert on your topic, your educational degrees (if they apply to the topic), work experience, and anything else you consider pertinent to the subject at hand. Include all of your achievements. See this as your résumé in prose, but make sure it's written specifically for your book.

Obviously an aspiring author who wants a deal with a traditional publisher needs to create an About the Author section for inclusion in a nonfiction proposal. However, a blogger needs a biography as well. Every blog should include an About the Author page. This allows readers to find out who you are and why you have the expertise to write your blog. This information gives your blog credibility.

So write your bio as part of the proposal process, and then copy and paste it on the "About" page of your blog. If you prefer to use a less formal bio for your blog, write it in the first-person tense using *I*. If you write your blog in a more formal voice, though, stick to third person for your "About" page as well.

Your Author Bio coupled with your Author Platform section provide vital information for acquisitions editors. These two pieces indicate if you can write your book and help sell it. As you weigh whether you are the right person to blog your book, you want to look at both of these sections as well.

AUTHOR'S PLATFORM:
LAYING THE GROUNDWORK FOR
A SUCCESSFUL BLOG AND BOOK

The publishing world has changed dramatically over the last decade. No longer can you simply present an agent or a publisher with a good idea and good writing and expect to get a contract in return. You must prove you are a good business partner. This means you have laid the groundwork for selling your book by creating an Author's Platform and prospective readers are ready and waiting to purchase your book as soon as the publisher releases it.

Platform equates to how many people you know or who know you in your target market and who will potentially buy your book. These people can be followers on Facebook; tweeple on Twitter; connections on LinkedIn; blog subscribers or readers; newsletter subscribers; podcast listeners; people reached via magazines, e-zines, and online publications for which you write; attendees at your talks and workshops; publicity partners; and fellow members of online and off-line associations. You build a platform through speaking, writing, social media activities, networking, and media gigs. You must build a platform before they will come—*they* meaning agents and publishers.

In today's publishing world, two of the most important parts of a book proposal are the Promotion and the Platform sections. Both show publishers that you can and will help sell your book, and the Promotion section relies on the Platform section for its success. Publishers want business partners, not just writers. Do you have your business hat on?

Why do you, a blogger or the writer of a blogged book, care about platform or the Platform section of a book proposal? First, if you want your blogged book to be discovered and turned into a printed book by a publishing house, you need platform. A publisher, and probably an agent, won't take you on without platform. Blog readers = platform (if enough of them exist). Second, if you would like to write another traditional book, or if you plan to produce a successful self-published print or digital version, then your blog serves as a way to promote that book and to build platform (i.e., potential buyers). Third, if you self-publish, you need platform to help sell your book(s), so you want to include this section in your proposal or business plan no matter what.

The more you build platform via guest blog posts on other blogs, articles published on your topic, news releases, press releases, e-zine articles, media appearances, talks, workshops, and, of course, a steady flow of blog posts, the more readers will show up at your blog. All of these efforts become platform elements. And the larger your platform, the higher your likelihood of producing a successful book—one that sells to publishers and to readers.

The Platform section of your book proposal includes a list of all the things you have done to date to develop an author platform. It includes statistics, such as how many unique visitors read your blog each day, how many page views you get daily on your website, how many places you have spoken in the last year or six months (and how many you have scheduled for the next six to twelve months), where you have appeared as a guest blogger, how many followers you have on Facebook, how many tweeple you have on Twitter, how many connections you have on LinkedIn, and how many people are on your mailing list.

Even if you don't write a proposal and produce a business plan for an indie book instead, it's a great idea to list these activities and statistics so you remember what you've done. It's also a good idea to keep track of these statistics so you can tell whether your readership and platform grow over time. Keep working on building your platform; don't let a month go by when you don't have some type of platform-building activity scheduled. In fact, you should do something to build platform every day.

By the way, the Platform section of a proposal can make or break an aspiring author's chance of getting a publishing deal. It's that important. So if your Platform section lacks entries, you'll want to begin working on it ASAP. Here are a few things you can do to build your platform quickly.

- Spend time every day on social networking activities.
- Begin speaking to groups interested in your subject matter.
- Join groups interested in your subject matter—or any groups (professional, networking, social). And get involved—volunteer and take on leadership roles.

- Write articles on your topic for online and print publications.
- Begin pitching to the media. Subscribe to www.HelpAReporter.com, PitchRate.com, and ReporterConnection.com and respond to the journalists' queries you will receive.
- Get active on social media sites (and share your posts).

MISSION STATEMENT: DO YOU FEEL COMPELLED TO BLOG YOUR BOOK?

If you decide to write a book proposal, you might want to include a Mission Statement section after your About the Author section. You've already worked on that. Remember the questions I asked in chapter three: "Why do you want to blog a book?" "What's your purpose?" "What's your mission?" and "What do you want to accomplish by writing this book?" The answers to those questions pertain here.

Not every book on writing a book proposal includes the Mission Statement section; in fact, many don't. However, my mentor and friend, Michael Larsen, who wrote *How to Write a Book Proposal*, asks his authors to include a Mission Statement, and such a section also appears in his own book. He says it gives writers a chance to write about their commitment to their book. Some place it at the beginning of their promotion plans as an expression of their commitment to sell books. I find it a really important section to include in a proposal or a business plan for an indie book.

I'll reiterate: Knowing why you feel compelled to blog or write this book helps you focus your energy on this project. It helps you clarify your reasons for blogging your book. It helps you decide if you *must* blog this book, and it helps the people considering purchasing your book (publishers and readers) decide if they *must* do so—if they *must* read it.

You can publish your Mission Statement on a page on your blog, too. This lets your blogged-book readers know why you feel compelled to write this blogged book. In this way you allow them to buy into your mission as well.

I've now covered all the sections included in what could be called the first half of a nonfiction proposal.

LIST OF CHAPTERS AND CHAPTER SUMMARIES: PLANNING YOUR POSTS OR CONTENTS IN SCREEN-SIZED PIECES

At this point in the planning process, you know what your blogged book is about and you've outlined its features and benefits. You know who is going to read it and in what markets you will promote it. You know the competition and how to differentiate your blogged book from other blogs and books already on the market. You're now ready to consider the contents of your book.

A blogged book must follow the guidelines of a blog—no long chapters here, only short 300- to 500-word posts. Most blog visitors want to read only approximately one computer screen's worth of copy.

Therefore your task involves coming up with what in book proposal terms is called the List of Chapters. This equates to the table of contents for your book and is the first of two sections included in what is sometimes called the Outline section of the proposal. However, you should have completed this in chapter three after the mind-mapping exercise. If not, you can do it now with a mind-mapping exercise like the one described previously or by brainstorming your topic.

Once you have created a table of contents for your book, reduce the chapters down into screen sized pieces comprised of all the subjects you came up with during mind mapping. You also can accomplish this task, or come up with more blog topics, by brainstorming with other people, doing research, or simply attempting another brain dump. What you want is a lengthy and detailed outline. Basically, you need to break each chapter into numerous smaller sections consisting of subtopics; the subtopics get labeled as subheadings in your chapters and serve as the titles to blog posts. Simply think about all the different topics you will cover in each chapter and give them titles; list them under the chapter title. (More on this exercise in chapter six.) Later, when you start blogging your book, each of these becomes a blog post.

To ensure you remember exactly what you are supposed to write when you are ready to compose the posts, take the time now also to write Chapter Summaries, the last section of the nonfiction book proposal. This entails composing a chapter-by-chapter synopsis, or a one- or two-paragraph description of the content, for each chapter. I suggest you also write a brief summary of each post, even if it's just one or two sentences. This will serve not only as a reminder (it's not unusual after a month or two to have forgotten what you had in mind for many of your posts) but also as a basic outline for each post. If you feel the title of the post (the subhead) will be enough of a reminder, go with it; in many cases that was enough for me.

Wow! Great job! You've completed the Author Training Process and compiled all the information you need for your blogged book's business plan or book proposal. Also, with your Overview, List of Chapters, and Chapter Summaries in hand, you have the best writing guide possible.

Before you can begin blogging your book, however, you need a blog. It's time to create your website so your book has a publishing home in cyberspace.

CHAPTER 5

CREATING YOUR BLOG

To begin writing and publishing the content of your book on the Internet, you must first create a website where your book will "live." The type of website you need is called a blog. Some people think of blogs as something other than "real" websites. In truth, blogs are very real, but they do operate a bit differently from traditional websites. (Sometimes they look different, too, and other times you can't tell the difference between a blog and a traditional website.) Better yet, some are free and all of them are relatively easy to use.

If you already have a website, you may consider including a self-hosted blog on that website. Most writers need a webmaster to set up a website and a self-hosted blog because it can be a complicated process. If you are technologically savvy, you may be able to create a self-hosted blog by yourself. You most certainly can create a free hosted blog alone. With the right software, you probably can do the maintenance on your website and run your blog. My webmaster set up my websites and blogs, and, for the most part, I do all the maintenance myself.

In my experience, many writers are a bit (if not more) technophobic. Plus, they don't want to be anything but writers. They definitely don't want to take the time to become webmasters or developers. Therefore, if you are like these other writers, using a blog platform that doubles as a website offers a perfect solution, whether you are first venturing into the world of blogging and website maintenance or have experience doing so. These days, many people have websites created with WordPress technology as well as blogs. They are easy to use and maintain if you know how to blog.

A typical blog functions as a system for managing your content—just like a website—as well as offering you an address, or home for that website, in cyberspace. It's an easy way to have control over your website. You can log in and add posts, pages, images, videos, and audio on your own without the need to pay a webmaster.

I'm not particularly technologically savvy. If I can manage a blog, so can you. You can create one, too. Even a technological delinquent like me can create a free hosted WordPress blog. I've done it several times, and it was reasonably easy to do.

HOSTED OR SELF-HOSTED? THAT IS THE QUESTION

If you don't understand the difference between WordPress.*com* free hosted blogs and WordPress.*org* self-hosted blogs, let me explain. (This explanation pertains to any type of free hosted vs. self-hosted blog. I am using WordPress as an example because this is the most commonly used blogging platform and the one I recommend.) WordPress.com, like other free blogging platforms, hosts your blog like a hosting company hosts your website. *Hosted* means the files and software used to build your website have somewhere to live on the Internet and you don't need to worry about maintaining the software that runs your blog. WordPress.com hosts blogs for millions of people. As the blogger, you are in control of the content, but your site resides at the WordPress location. That means that the traffic you generate—the readers who show up to read your blogged book—show up at YourBloggedBook.WordPress.com, for example. Having a free hosted blog with any blogging platform is a bit like housing it in a commune or an apartment building. Everyone shares the same address.

WordPress.org, on the other hand, is free software you download and install on your own Web host. You pay a minimal fee per year (on average about $100 for basic service) from a hosting company of your choice, such as www.Bluehost.com, www.HostGator.com, or www.A2hosting.com, but your blog lives at the location you choose at a specific address on the Internet where you and you alone reside. Your blog or website is the sole tenant living at that residence; no other blog has the same address.

I've had free hosted blogs both on www.Blogger.com and on WordPress.com. Other hosted blogging companies exist, such as www.Typepad.com and www.Tumblr.com; check them out as well, if you like. WordPress has become the most widely used and accepted blogging platform.

I prefer WordPress.org. In my experience, it offers more options and gives you more exposure. I immediately had more traffic to my blog when I switched from www.Blogger.com to WordPress.org, and I could actually find my blog when I searched for it on Google. I couldn't find my Blogger blog when I searched for it, which doesn't make a lot of sense since Blogger is part of Google. Google's chief of search engine results, Matt Cutts, recommends WordPress. Enough said!

I also have several self-hosted blogs—four in all—with WordPress. org, which webmasters have set up for me. All but two of them began as free hosted WordPress.com blogs. (Notice the difference: WordPress. com = free and hosted by WordPress; WordPress.org = fee based and self-hosted by you.) In the last five years, my webmaster converted all my free hosted blogs to self-hosted blogs. It's best to start out hosting your own blogs because it saves you the trouble and the expense of converting to self-hosted blogs later. It also saves you the decision of what to do with the old free hosted blogs after you convert them to self-hosted blogs. WordPress.com lets you delete them, make them private, or forward the old address to a new one. I didn't want to just delete mine because this can sometimes cause problems with the new hosted blog. I didn't want to make them private because they remain visible on the Internet for readers to find; plus, those who do find them get a message saying they are private. I didn't want to leave them up and running, although that's what ended up happening until I realized they were taking traffic away from my self-hosted WordPress.org blogs and readers were still leaving comments there. Now I pay $12 per year to have the old hosted WordPress.com blog addresses forwarded to my new self-hosted WordPress.org addresses. (If I could do it over again, I'd start with self-hosted blogs and save myself that $36 per year I now pay in forwarding fees for three blogs.)

If you can't afford to self-host your blog, however, the free hosted ones work well until you're ready to convert—or forever if you so choose. Self-hosted blogs do offer you more options and visibility, plus they ensure that the traffic you garner goes to your own website and not to a common website. Some of the better website hosting companies will allow you to host more than one site (blog) on one plan for just a few cents more each month, should you become a multiple blog owner like me.

If you don't know anything about hosting or about HTML codes (and you don't want to learn), you may want to stick with a free hosted blog. Self-hosting your own installation of any blogging software may provide you with additional flexibility and design options, but this only has benefit if you are willing to learn how to use it or if you can afford a webmaster or developer to at least set it up for you. (Hiring someone to create your site can run from a few hundred dollars—if you hire someone on oDesk, for example—to several thousand dollars, depending on your needs. The average blog setup costs between $1,000 and $3,000 if you hire a seasoned developer.) Then you can just write, post, and do simple maintenance.

Once the blog is designed and "live," you can manage it yourself. I promise. Many website hosting companies offer the option to start with WordPress-hosted sites, thereby eliminating the need for installations of any kind, though you will still have to maintain the Word-Press software by installing updates from time to time. Usually the updating process is as simple as the click of a button.

The process of setting up a hosted blog is fairly self-explanatory. If you are having trouble with either a hosted blog or a self-hosted blog, I suggest you hire a webmaster or blogging professional to help you. If possible, find one that offers online tutorials in the blogging platform you have chosen.

You can find more information on blog construction in some great books on the market. Keep in mind that some of them were released a while ago and may need an update.

1. *WordPress: The Missing Manual* by Matthew MacDonald
2. *WordPress for Beginners: A Visual Step-by-Step Guide to Creating Your Own WordPress Site in Record Time, Starting from Zero!* by Dr. Andy Williams

3. *WordPress to Go: How to Build a WordPress Website on Your Own Domain, from Scratch, Even If You Are a Complete Beginner* by Sarah McHarry

4. *WordPress Websites Step-by-Step: The Complete Beginner's Guide to Creating a Website or Blog with WordPress* by Caimin Jones

5. *Blogging for Dummies* by Susannah Gardner and Shane Birley

6. *The Complete Idiot's Guide to Creating a Web Page & Blog* by Paul McFedries

7. *WordPress for Dummies* by Lisa Sabin-Wilson and Matt Mullenweg

The hosted blog sites lead you through the set-up process fairly effortlessly. And while this is not meant to be a how-to-create-a-self-hosted-blog manual, I will discuss several steps to setting up your blog.

PURCHASING A DOMAIN NAME

Whether or not you plan on having a self-hosted blog, you should purchase a domain name for your blogged book. (Purchasing a domain name typically costs under $10; the price goes down if you purchase it for two or more years.) Your blogged book's domain name is its address in cyberspace. Should you convert from a hosted blog to a self-hosted one, you'll need a domain name. (You may want to forward your old hosted blog to the new self-hosted blog's address, as I did.) If you begin with a self-hosted blog, you'll need the domain name to get started. Be sure to purchase the exact same domain name as the title of your blogged book.

While you're at it, purchase a domain name that reflects your own name as an author. For example, I own NinaAmir.com as well as HowToBlogABook.com. You can direct this domain name to your blogged book's website. People who don't know the name of your blogged book (or who have forgotten it) may search for you by name and find your blog in this manner. Or you may want to create an author's website at some point; having the domain name (and ensuring that someone else doesn't purchase it) will come in handy. You might even purchase the domain name that reflects a character, place, unique phrase, or new brand you have created that exists only in your book. Consider also buying domain names that reflect other search terms that might direct readers to your blogged book. For example, I also own BloggingRelief.com, BloggingForAuthors.com, BlogYour WayToABookDeal.com, and BuildABusinessAroundYourBlog.com.

If you can't get a .com name (e.g., HowToBlogABook.com), get a .net name (e.g., HowToBlogABook.net). These are the second most common type of domain name. If you can't get one of these two, pick one of the others, such as .info, .org, or .tv, or even .me. Some people purchase every domain name possible so no one else can purchase them. This becomes a bit costly, since each domain name has a yearly fee attached to it. I do recommend purchasing .com, .net, and .org, since these are the most common. (Some people think there is a large distinction between the different types of domain names, such as .org and .com. In truth, there is not. It is true that .org usually is used by organizations, however.)

You can purchase domain names in any number of places. The cost varies, so do your research. Many places, like www.GoDaddy.com and www.Namecheap.com, offer cheap rates, and some also provide hosting. You can do a Google search and then comparison shop.

CHOOSING A THEME

The way your blog, website, or blogged book looks depends on the theme you choose. When you sign up for a free hosted blog, you can search through the numerous themes offered and download one. Find the "Theme" option under the "Appearance" menu in the dashboard on WordPress.com. The same holds true for a WordPress self-hosted blog. Additionally, you can find more free—and not free—themes on various Internet sites. First check out WordPress.org to find thousands of free available themes. You are likely to discover something that suits you and your needs there. (The direct address is WordPress.org/extend/themes.) Simply Google "WordPress themes" or "free WordPress themes" to find them. You will pay for the best "optimized" themes, such as the Genesis Framework by Wordpress.

I find choosing a theme the most time-consuming part of setting up a new blog. There are so many from which to choose! And they don't all work the same way. Some are search engine optimized; some are not. Some are widget ready; some are not. Some are complicated; some are simple. Some are pretty; some are ugly. Some are interesting; some are boring. A blog theme exists for every blogger's personality, that's for sure. I've been known to download one and think it's perfect only to discover it is too difficult for me to use or it has one strange hitch I dislike. That sends me back to search for a new theme all over again.

If you find that choosing a theme sends you over the edge, you may simply be overthinking your theme decision. Someone once told me good blog content always outweighs blog design. Take a deep breath, and take a break. Then pick one of the themes you've tested and use it for a while. You can always try another one later.

If you can't see doing any or all of this yourself, hire a WordPress expert, or developer, to design your blog from scratch. This takes only as long as the time needed to describe your blogged book, how you envision your blog and website, how many pages you need, and other basics. I recommend this path. While you begin writing the first posts to your blogged book, the developer will create your blog. You might have to sign off on the theme he chooses, but it then will be modified in a variety of ways to suit your needs or your fancy. You then only write one more thing: a check. The advantage to this method, which I must admit I have employed for all but one of my blogs, is that your blog, website, and blogged book appear unique. No one but you will ever have this exact blog design. (Yes, other sites might use the same theme, but your site will look somewhat different because of the modifications made.) Also, your site will have many of the professional touches you need, as well as the best themes, for visibility and efficiency.

In any event, don't let your difficulty choosing a template or theme keep you from getting started. In the beginning, nobody reads or searches for your blogged book anyway. Use the default template if you must and make changes to the theme later when you have some readers and more experience blogging.

MANAGING YOUR BLOG MENUS

Your blog will have a lot of different menus. I'm not going to discuss all of them, but I will mention a few important ones.

First, let's focus on the "Settings" menu. In this area you give your blogged book its title and subtitle and ensure that its URL, or domain name, and your name and contact information are all displayed correctly.

Sticking again with the WordPress blogging program, under "Settings," click on "General." There you will see a place to fill in your "Site Title." This is your blogged book's title. Underneath this, fill in the blank for "Tagline" with your subtitle. These both appear on the blog. In some cases your subtitle may be too long and will not look good in the blog's theme. You may need to pick another theme or shorten the subtitle for use on the blog.

Next, in the space for "WordPress Address" and "Site Address," add your domain name without "http://www" before it. For example, MyBloggedBook.com.

Fill in the "Email Address" space with whatever e-mail address you want to use. Comments will go to this address.

Now go to the "Discussions" menu under "Settings," and under "Default Article Settings" choose "Allow link notifications from other blogs (pingbacks and trackbacks)" and "Allow people to post comments on new articles." This means you will be notified if other bloggers mention your blog posts and your readers can comment on your posts. If you mention other blogs, or include links to them, in posts, and you want those sites notified, choose "Attempt to notify any blogs linked to from the article."

In the following section, "Other Comment Settings," choose "Comment author must fill out name and email," and "Enable threaded (nested) comments __ levels deep." This means you've asked those readers who want to comment to leave a name and an e-mail address so you know who they are and can contact them. And you've enabled a stream of comments to form on one post.

If you want to be notified when readers comment, in the next section, "Email me whenever," choose "Anyone posts a comment." You can also choose to be notified if a comment is held for moderation.

Whether or not you want to moderate all comments is up to you as well. Choose this in the next section, "Before a comment appears." Adjust "Comment moderation" only if you have specific spam concerns.

Last, under the "Privacy" menu, which also resides under "Settings," be sure to click on the option "I would like my site visible to everyone including search engines and archives." This makes it possible for your blogged book to be found on Google, Yahoo, Bing, etc.

The rest of the general settings area should be self-explanatory.

Now go to the "Users" menu, and under that heading click on "Your Profile." Here, be sure to write in "admin" in the blank for "Username"—you are the administrator of the blog—and to type in your name or whatever name you choose in the blank for "Nickname." I suggest you use your first or first and last name for this so when you reply to a blog comment, readers will know it's you, the author of the blogged book.

When it comes to writing, WordPress allows you to create what it calls "authors." This helps you distinguish your blogging tasks. If you don't want to do maintenance on your blog, for instance, you may want an author login and password rather than (or in addition to) an administrator login and password. You can then log in with this and write like a mad thing and not have to worry about anything else going on with the website or blog. You won't be distracted from doing what you should be doing—writing. You can leave website or blog maintenance to someone else, such as a webmaster or developer. Or you can log in as the administrator at any time to do something other than write.

Having an author and an administrator account also is considered a good security practice because websites can be accessed by other people, or "hacked." Passwords on administration accounts can sometimes be weak—don't just use a form of the word "administrator."

Under "Display Name Publicly," be sure to choose how you want your name displayed. Also you can add a website, if you have one other than the blog itself, and fill in the other form fields, including a short bio.

CHOOSING PLUGINS AND WIDGETS

Once you have your blog set up, you can add many automated features. However, this ability is severely curtailed if you have a free hosted blog—another reason to opt for a self-hosted blog. You can choose from all sorts of fancy and not-so-fancy widgets and plugins. These add tools, features, and automatization to your site, including such things as search boxes, archives, search engine optimization, backup tools, and ways to "ping" your posts to social networking sites and garner e-mail subscribers. You can pick and choose which ones you like and want to use.

Widgets allow bloggers who don't possess coding knowledge to modify the design and content of their sites using a simple point-and-click or drag-and-drop system. Often, a plugin will create a new widget you need or want. Plugins add features to your site that expand and automate its functionality. You simply download plugins to your blog, activate them, and use them. (You can search for them even if you don't know the exact name of a particular plugin.) Once loaded to the site as a plugin, widgets are found under the "Appearance" menu. Plugins are a stand-alone menu.

If you want a particular tool to serve your blogged book, you can bet someone has created a plugin that will do it for you. When searching for plugins, look at their ratings to judge their effectiveness. Choose wisely. You might also do a Google search to see what others might say about those particular tools. Notice if a particular plugin is being updated frequently; if not, choose another.

Keep in mind that when you apply a plugin, it may change your theme. Not all plugins are compatible with all themes. I added one to HowToBlogABook.com that I use on all my other blogs, and it produced four lines of odd coding; I had to deactivate it. Then I added another plugin and, after deactivating it, found that my blog was suddenly "unavailable" because I hadn't removed the inactive plugin. (Don't panic if something like this happens. Do some research on Google. Inevitably someone else has had the same experience and solved the problem.)

You will find as many opinions about plugins and widgets as there are blog developers. Based on a survey of those I trust, combined with my own experience, here's my list of recommended plugins and widgets.

The most important widgets to add to a blog are:

- **ARCHIVES** or **MOST RECENT POSTS:** archives all your past posts, sorted by month/date/year, depending on which archive widget you get; if you have many years of posts, consider just featuring the most recent or popular posts
  - This widget is included with WordPress.
  - Create a recent or popular post listing with a plugin like **CUSTOM RECENT POSTS WIDGET, EXTENSIVE RECENT POSTS WIDGET, OR WP POPULAR POSTS.**
- **CATEGORIES:** allows (or provides) organization, or filing, of posts by subject matter
  - This widget is included with WordPress.
- **SUBSCRIBE:** allows readers to subscribe to your posts; best to use RSS-to-e-mail via a paid e-mail marketing service like MailChimp or Aweber than to use the free FeedBurner service since the future of that service, which is provided by Google, is uncertain; consider also having one for subscriptions to an e-mail list

The most important plugins to consider adding are:

- **WORDPRESS SEO BY YOAST:** allows you to write a short description of your post, add a keyword or keyword phrase, and check to see if the post has good SEO
- **SHARING TOOLS** (such as **SOCIAL SHARING TOOLKIT, DIGG DIGG** or **JETPACK**): allows readers to share, bookmark, and e-mail your posts and pages using any service, such as Facebook, Twitter, Google Plus, StumbleUpon, Digg, and many more
- **AKISMET:** comes with your WordPress install, but be sure to set up an account on the Akismet website to activate this "captcha" plugin and to protect your blog from comment and trackback spam; you might need a better captcha plugin later as you get more traffic

- **GROWMAP ANTI SPAMBOT** or **BAD BEHAVIOR:** additional comment spam filters; these days Akismet is not enough to handle the amount that might come your way
- **GOOGLE XML SITEMAPS:** generates a special XML sitemap which helps search engines like Google, Yahoo, Bing, and Ask to better index your blog, but you don't need it if you use WordPress SEO by Yoast
- **GOOGLE ANALYTICS:** free site analytics that allow you to track your unique visitors, page views, bounce rate, and much more
- **GOOGLE ANALYTICATOR** or **GOOGLE ANALYTICS BY YOAST:** enables Google Analytics on your blog; be sure you have the new Google Universal Analytics set up for your site vs. the old Google Analytics
- **WP-DBMANAGER** or **BACKUPBUDDY:** manages and schedules backup of your WordPress database; makes sure backups are being saved in the cloud
- **DISQUS:** a comment moderation system that replaces WordPress's built-in comment moderation system with a more widely accessible comment feature set; offers a remote comment system that allows you to log in using social networks, like Facebook, Twitter, etc.
- **WP-CACHE** or **W3 TOTAL CACHE:** recommended for sites that get a lot of traffic to speed up downloading time for your readers
- **SUCURI:** protects your site from hackers
- **CONTACT FORM 7:** creates a contact form on your site
- **TINYMCE ADVANCED EDITOR:** provides options for font sizes, fonts, and other things missing in the WordPress editor
- **SUBSCRIBE TO COMMENTS:** allows readers to engage with you by being kept informed of replies to their comments on the blog, thus creating a conversation
- **CAPTCHA:** cuts down on the spam by requiring input of a code prior to submitting a blog comment

ADDITIONAL PLUGINS NECESSARY FOR BLOGGED BOOKS

Blogs that host blogged books have a few additional needs, such as a way to "turn pages" and to show readers the entire book you have built or are building on the site. You may want to direct visitors to a table of contents so they can find the "first page" and begin reading. From there, readers will want to click through to the next post (and the next and the next) until they reach the end. Such functions and features require additional plugins.

Here are some suggested plugins for blogged-book sites.

- **WP POST NAVIGATION:** gives you facility to show "Previous" and "Next Post" links at the top or bottom of a post
- **ADMIN POST NAVIGATION:** adds links to navigate to the next and previous posts when editing a post in the WordPress admin account
- **GENESIS POST NAVIGATION:** adds "Previous" and "Next Post" links on a single post with the post title; allows customization of the post navigation colors and provides an option to navigate posts within a category; requires Genesis framework
- **TABLE OF CONTENTS PLUS:** automatically creates a customizable table of contents and outputs a sitemap listing pages and/or categories across your entire site
- **WP TABLE OF PAGINATED CONTENTS:** allows you to name posts and pages to create a table of contents; offers choices of a list or drop-down menu using next- and previous-post page navigation
- **SIMPLE TOC:** allows the creation of multiple wiki-like tables of contents using shortcode

Try out each plugin, and see which ones serve your needs best. Remember, new plugins are created all the time, and sometimes the old ones are not updated often enough. So choose wisely.

Keep in mind that too many plugins can slow a site down, and unused ones should be deleted, as they pose a security risk.

INSTALLING ANALYTICS

One of the most important tools you want to add to your site is an analytics program. The free hosted WordPress.com sites have basic analytics. This allows you to see how much traffic comes to your blog, what pages are the most popular, and where most of your visitors come from. You cannot use Google Universal Analytics on a free hosted WordPress blog.

For self-hosted blogs, choose from any number of free analytics available, but I recommend Google Universal Analytics, which is the industry standard. Your hosting company may also have analytics (free or fee based). I use both Google Universal Analytics (formerly Google Analytics) and the AWStats program provided by my hosting company. Note that their statistics tend to differ enormously, because they track in very different ways. Most experts I've asked agree that AWStats tends to overstate numbers and that Google Analytics understates them. So your true statistics are probably somewhere in the middle.

Once you have analytics installed on your blog, you can tell how many readers are visiting your site. It won't be as many as you would like, especially at first. Educate yourself on the difference between a *hit*, a *visitor*, a *unique visitor*, and a *page view*. I'm going to spend some time on this, because most people do not understand it. As a blogger and an author of a blogged book, you *need* to understand it (even if you really don't *want* to understand it) so you can talk about your blog statistics in an educated manner. Why? So you can tell an agent or acquisitions editor about your platform and provide the correct statistics when they ask—which they did when I was negotiating my contract for this book. I had offered hits in my proposal because this is the largest number. (I knew it wasn't the most important.) Later, after the proposal was accepted and we were negotiating the contract, the sales and marketing team asked me for unique visitor and page view counts because these are the numbers that really matter. (This is where your AWStats numbers might be nice to have ...) So here we go. (Don't let your eyes glaze over.)

Technically a *hit* is each file sent to a browser by a Web server; therefore, it's not a visitor, or reader, of any type. It's anything on the page of your blogged book that gets sent to a browser—a photo, content, a logo, a post.

A *visitor* is a browser that accepts a *cookie*, or small script. Let's say you visit a website. A cookie then is placed on the hard drive of your computer by the server of that website. The cookie is used to recognize your specific browser/computer combination if you return to the same site. If a cookie is not accepted, an IP number or address, which is like an online fingerprint, will track your browser/computer combination. Each Internet connection has its own IP number or address, which is a bit like your home address in cyberspace. IP addresses on any network are a single device, but they can be a single IP address shared by a number of computers. Therefore, a single IP address in your website log may not represent just one person.

A visitor could be an actual reader or a crawler, spider, or bot—all of those "things" that search engines use to catalog websites and content.

The all-important *unique visitor* refers to an actual unduplicated person—not bots, crawlers, or spiders (and not a hit)—coming to your website over the course of a specified time period: twenty-four hours. Different from a site's hits or page views, which are measured by the number of files requested from a particular site, unique visitors are recognized and measured by cookies they accepted previously (unbeknownst to them) and by their unique IP addresses. Also, they are counted only once no matter how many times they visit the site during that time period—unless they delete the cookie from their computer and then return to the site. In this case, they will get a new cookie and be counted again. Thus, in simple terms, a unique visitor is someone who visits your site once in a given time period.

A *visit* occurs when someone or something (possibly a bot) visits your site. It consists of one or more page views or hits. One visitor can generate multiple site visits.

Page views are generated each time a visitor views a page on your website, regardless of how many hits are created at the same time. Pages are comprised of files, and every image in a page is a separate file. Readers look at a blogged-book page, or a blog post, thus creating a page view. They may see numerous images, graphics, or pictures, and all of these generate multiple hits. One page view can create hundreds of hits, which is why page views are more important than hits.

Your *bounce rate* indicates if a visitor interacts with more than one page during a visit. Technically, it's the percentage of single-page sessions that occur, or the number of times a person leaves your site from the same page they entered without interacting with the page. This could happen if they arrive, find the information they need (read that blog post), and leave because they have no need or interest in going to other pages.

Now that you understand how to tell if you have readers, it's time to start creating something for people to read: your blogged book. This gives the visitors a reason to come to your website or blog. Then you can watch your analytics and wait for readers to arrive. As you keep writing, you'll be able to watch the numbers grow.

XML SITEMAPS AND BLOG REGISTRATION

After you have created your blog, you need to verify it with Google, the largest of all the search engines. For this you need an XML sitemap, which essentially provides a map of an entire website. This helps your site get discovered. Don't confuse an XML sitemap with an HTML sitemap, which is used by the "Search" widget.

You can create an XML sitemap using Google Webmaster Tools for any publicly viewable site that has been claimed with Google. Before Google Sites will generate an XML sitemap, however, you must verify your site with Google Webmaster Tools. You can complete both steps here: www.google.com/webmasters/tools/home.

The easiest way to create an XML sitemap, however, is with a plugin, such as WordPress SEO by Yoast or XML Sitemaps. MaAnna Stephenson of BlogAid provided these steps for submitting one to Google Webmaster Tools, but you also can submit your XML sitemap manually to other search engines.

1. Connect Google Analytics to your site via a plugin, like Google Analytics by Yoast or the Google Analyticator plugin. (One of the easiest tricks for verifying your site on Google Webmaster Tools is using the analytics code.)
2. Create the XML sitemap with the WordPress SEO by Yoast plugin. There is a button that allows you to view your XML sitemap. Copy the URL shown.

3. Verify your site on Google Webmaster Tools using the analytics code.
4. Submit your XML sitemap on Google Webmaster Tools by inputting the slug of the URL you copied.

Please note that this brief tutorial omits additional steps in each process. Also, some debate exists among developers about whether Google Webmaster Tools should be used by those with little or no knowledge of such things. An inexperienced blogger can do a host of damage to a site using Google Webmaster Tools if he or she doesn't complete the XML sitemap and Google verification process correctly, including completely delisting it from Google. It is best to hire an expert, such as a developer or WordPress pro, to do this job for you.

YOU NEED PAGES

Before you begin writing your blogged book, take a little time to create some additional pages on your site besides the actual blog page. This becomes especially important if you plan to use your blog as your website. In other words, if your blog isn't self-hosted on an actual website and it serves as your website, you want to add pages in addition to those that feature the actual blogged book.

Pages are easy to add in WordPress.com or WordPress.org. On the left side of your blog dashboard you'll see a menu that says "Pages." Underneath this, the menu has an option to "Add new." Click on this. You then are given a menu to add a new page.

Title the first new page "About the Author." (If you took the time to go through the proposal process in chapter four, you have already created a bio. Use it here.) Since you are writing a book, you want readers to know the author. In particular, you want acquisitions editors and literary agents who drop by to know who you are. Write your author's bio in a professional manner. I like the ones written in the third person, just like in a book proposal. However, if you are writing your book in an informal tone, you might want to write your bio in the first person. Lots of bloggers include witty and informal "About" or "About the Author" pages, even if they aren't blogging a book, and these personal bios are recommended for blogs. Include a photo of yourself taken by a professional as well.

Next create an "About This Blog" page. Tell your readers why you began writing your blog. Consider including the Mission Statement or part or all of the Overview that you wrote during the proposal process in chapter four, especially the part about the benefits of reading the blogged book. Let your readers know why you feel compelled to write your blogged book and what they will gain by becoming loyal blog followers. Help them buy into your blog by including your Mission Statement.

You may want to include a "Media Kit" page. On this page include a shorter bio with a link to a longer bio, a downloadable photo, topics upon which you can speak, and links to questions the media can ask you on your topic. If you already speak on your topic (and you should), list the names of your speeches. You also may want a page specifically dedicated to your speaking activities—such as a "Hire Me to Speak" page where you can list upcoming and past speaking engagements.

Include a "Contact Me" page with a contact form. Do not include your e-mail address; doing so increases spam and the risk of getting hacked.

If you offer services of some sort or sell anything, you can add "Products and Services" pages.

You can add as many pages as you like, or as many as the theme you have chosen will permit, but be sure that if they are listed underneath the banner at the top of the home page of the blog you don't create so many that you run out of space. The most important pages to include are those that pertain to you, the author, and your blogged book. Second in importance are your media or speaking pages, so be sure that information has been included as well. Whatever doesn't fit at the top of the blog page can be added on the sidebar or nestled as drop-down menus discovered if a visitor hovers over the main pages, depending on your theme.

If your blog is self-hosted on a static website, many, if not all, of these pages can be included on your website rather than on the blog itself. These days, most people are ridding themselves of static websites, however, and moving totally to blog sites. So consider having your whole website created with WordPress.

Finally, you are ready to begin writing your blogged book one post at a time in cyberspace.

CHAPTER 6

WRITING YOUR BLOGGED BOOK

Okay! Let's start writing that blogged book!

Writing a blogged book is a bit different from writing a manuscript for a printed book because blogging lends itself to informality, brevity, and immediacy. When blogging, you can write in short bits and pieces as if composing e-mails to a friend. You don't ponder over your writing for days and weeks; you write, edit, and publish. The process is quick, and the whole book manuscript comes together quickly. Sometimes, short e-books come together in a similar fashion.

As I said before, blogs began as live journals, and many people considered them streams of consciousness—simply unedited thoughts thrown together and published. I'm not suggesting you go to that extreme with your book. Carefully choose your words and edit your copy before you send your posts into cyberspace. Put your best words forward—up to a point. You don't want to become a perfectionist as this will deter you from publishing posts frequently.

Consider your blogged book your first or second draft. Don't get upset if you discover you have gotten off track, left something out, made a mistake, or need to change, add, or delete copy. Assuming you have blogged-book readers, you do, indeed, make your errors and foibles public. However, if you don't stumble too often, it isn't a problem. Plus, you can avoid this issue almost entirely by planning out your book well (see chapter three) and working on your blog copy offline prior to publishing posts, a process I'll cover later in this chapter.

Blogging software makes it easy to edit posts, delete posts, and insert new posts into the "stream" of your book. Thus, I don't consider errors much of a deterrent to blogging a book. You can correct most of them when you discover them.

Remember, you can think of your blogged book as a test-market version of your printed book. Know that before the printed book gets published you have another chance to edit, revise, and add to it—to create a final draft. The initial blogged version does not have to be perfect, and hopefully you'll find that fact creatively freeing. Blogging a book is simply about getting your thoughts down quickly, in short bursts and pieces, on a regular schedule without the need for perfection.

While you compose your book, keep in mind that you are blogging. The beauty of blogging lies in the fact that it allows you to write about what's in your heart or mind at any moment or on any particular day. As you blog your book, you may find yourself going off on a tangent. Perhaps you feel moved to write about something related to your topic that's not in your table of contents. Or maybe you decide to take a day or two to discuss something that simply feels important to you. That's okay. In fact, it's great. As you'll read in chapter eleven, the bloggers featured there who booked their blogs and received publishing contracts all simply blogged. None of them set out to blog a book. Their books were organic products of good blogging. So, first and foremost, be a good blogger. However, set out with a plan. Know where you are going and want to end up. This way you'll produce the content you need for your book—and maybe some extra content as well.

I set up Google Alerts on subjects related to my book. (You can easily do this by signing into your Google Plus account and then clicking on the little grid that features all the Google products. Click on "more" and then "even more." A new screen will appear in your browser. Scroll down until you see "Specialized Search"; there you will find "Alerts." You also can go to the Google search engine and search for "Google Alert" and then follow the directions.) I continue to receive daily notifications about things like blog-to-book deals or industry studies related to blogging and blogs turned into books. In many cases, these may affect what I write about on my blog and, while I was blogging the book, often inspired me to blog on new subjects that were not on my already lengthy list of planned subjects.

Sometimes in the midst of writing, another idea came to me or I realized I had totally forgotten about an important step in the book-blogging process. I then wrote that blog post. If I realized this step needed to be inserted earlier in the book, I moved it to the appropriate "date," or I just let my readers know it should have come earlier in the book (or several days earlier in the blog).

Occasionally I offered a "commercial break." If I had a workshop or teleseminar coming up, I'd actually tell my readers about it in a blog post as well.

As with any writing process, when I blog a book I don't stay tethered to my outline. I let it be exactly that—an outline. I stay pretty close to its structure, but the outline grows and changes as I write.

Feel free to write—to blog! Don't ever let the book blogging, or the planning you've done, become a constraint. Allow it to open your creative flow.

CREATING YOUR BLOGGED-BOOK CONTENT

Hopefully you took the time in chapter four to create your List of Chapters (table of contents) and to write your Chapter Summaries (chapter-by-chapter synopsis). If not, I suggest you do so now. This provides a starting point for any book. Remember, you are, indeed, writing a book even if you intend to blog it.

As I suggested in chapter four, break down each chapter's subject into as many subheads, or subtopics, as you can think of at this time. These become the different blog posts you write, each one averaging about 300 to 500 words in length. If you were writing a full-length chapter for a printed nonfiction book, you would break it up with subheads anyway. Some novels or memoirs also break chapters into sections. Most chapters have at least four or five subheadings. For a blogged book, you need more. Depending on the length of your chapter, you may need ten or twenty subheads (post titles). Write them as catchy titles someone will want to read. Lots of blogs include lists, such as "Five Ways to Skin a Cat" or "Ten Tips for Success," or questions, such as "How Do I Use Twitter?" or "Is It Possible to Find an Agent?"

Although you wrote many, if not all, of your chapter and post titles in chapter four, now reconsider their titles as you think about how you will set up your blog categories. Categories are used to catalog the subject of your posts and typically are listed in the sidebar of your blog so readers can find posts on particular topics. Will your categories be filed by chapter titles? Or will you use the subjects about which you have written? Subjects are better for SEO and simple for reader searches. But your category listing could get quite long if you include every subject you've written about in each chapter. It's best to keep your category listing on the short side; some people say ten to fifteen topics is enough. You can add subtopics within each category to divide topics further, but some experts frown upon this practice.

After you create your subheads (blog post titles), consider the content you want to include in each of these smaller chapter sections. Each blog post will be only about three or four paragraphs long.

One way to come up with both titles and content involves devising five or ten questions that you plan to answer in each chapter, or in parts of your chapter. The questions become blog post titles. The answers to these questions become your content as you compose blog posts. When you edit your manuscript into a book, you can change the questions into transition sentences that begin each paragraph, or you can write an introduction to the section itself and delete the questions. (You'll probably need an introductory paragraph for each section anyway.) Some people use the questions as additional subheadings. I don't advocate this approach because I don't find it interesting to read a book full of questions and answers. The questions do work well as blog post titles, however, since search engines tend to like questions.

Another way to come up with a list of blog posts entails writing "keyword sentences" for topics under each of your chapter subheads. These can function like transitions between paragraphs in your posts but primarily serve to remind you what to write about. You also might use actual keywords, or search terms, that search engines can find in these sentences (more on this later). Right now we are mainly concerned with words that focus you on the subject at hand when it's time to write your posts. Begin by writing a sentence that lets you and the reader know what topic will be covered. The rest of the paragraph elaborates on this. You can create a keyword sentence with a full statement, with a few words, or by asking yourself questions. You can delete these writing prompts afterward and simply make sure all copy flows well. This makes for much more interesting writing than including questions, as I mentioned before. If you wrote a strong keyword sentence that flowed well into your subsequent blog post, however, you can include it.

If you look at the previous paragraph, for example, you can see that the first sentence functions as a keyword sentence.

> Another way to come up with a list of blog posts entails writing "keyword sentences" for topics under each of your chapter subheads.

This keyword sentence also employs some search engine keywords and keyword phrases: *blog, blog posts, writing, keyword sentences, keyword, chapter subheads, subheads,* and *topics.*

If I had put a subhead, or post title, on this section it might have read:

How to Use Keyword Sentences to Create Chapter Subheadings

As you write, you will think of other posts to add under your subheadings or subtopics. You may even add more subtopics with additional posts. As I blogged this book, I came up with many additional topics. Again, allow yourself to be a blogger and a writer. Add more content as the inspiration hits you. Hopefully you'll have days when you get in the flow and new topics come to mind. It's good to have a springboard (your outline or plan) from which to start, however.

As I began editing and revising the manuscript for *How to Blog a Book,* I added even more content I felt I'd left out of the first draft. Keep in mind that as you blog your book you produce a *first draft,* not a final draft, of your book. Of course, you will polish each post as much as possible before you hit the publish button, but your blogged book will not be a perfect or finished version of your book. Remember that, and it should free you to write and publish quickly and easily. Don't let your Inner Perfectionist take hold of you and stop you from publishing your work on the Internet.

HOW TO COMPOSE YOUR BLOG POSTS

Compose your book as a manuscript written in Microsoft Word, or some other word processing program, and not in your blog program. In other words, don't write your book in WordPress, Typepad, or Blogger, hit publish, and consider this your manuscript. By creating an actual manuscript in Word, you have a version to later edit when it comes time to produce a printed or digital book. You do, indeed, want to have a complete manuscript from which to work.

If you have not created a manuscript while blogging your book, you will then have to copy and paste all your blog posts from your site to create one. And that's all you'll have on your actual blog—individual posts—not a continuous set of posts that can be copied as one long document. Compiling those posts is a *huge* job you want to avoid. Plus, a manuscript gives you a backup of your hard work. Your blog should be providing a backup of all your posts (see the list of plugins in chapter five), but the more backups the better.

There are only two tools I've discovered that can help you move posts from a blog into Word: Blog Book Maker (BlogBookMaker.com) and Blog Booker (BlogBooker.com). Find out more in chapter seven.

By creating a manuscript, you have the ability to see your book being created before your eyes in a more traditional manner as well. In a word processing program you can run a word count. You can move posts around and see them all together in sequence. You can print out the document and read a hard copy. You can even put it in a binder, place dividers between the chapters, and get the tangible and visual sense that you are, indeed, writing a book. You also can work with editors and get them to provide feedback on the hard copy of the manuscript.

If you prefer, you can write your posts in your blogging software and then copy and paste them into Microsoft Word after publishing them rather than before. Some people feel more like bloggers if they write in their blogging program. Doing so can give you a better sense of a "screen's worth of copy." It's pretty easy to preview your post and see how it looks on your computer screen, and this can feel fun and exciting.

A screen's worth of copy consists of a printed page's worth, or 250 words—more if you choose—of content. Some bloggers write 1,000-word posts if they only post once a week. This also is okay for what are called long-tail posts. These are much like evergreen articles, ones readers come back to again and again because the topics never get old or because people search for them on the Internet over and over again. These will drive traffic to your blog day and night even though you wrote them long ago. I wrote one like this for my blog *My Son Can Dance* on how to wear a dance belt. (You'd be amazed at how many people search for information on dance belts and how to wear them.) However, most of your posts should be within the 300- to 500-word range. You don't have to do a word count every time, but keep in mind that every 700-word post you write could be two day's worth of posts rather than one. That's a large incentive to break that post into two, if you ask me.

Like anything else you write, a post should have a beginning, a middle, and an end. In the case of blogging a book, though, this is all the more important because your posts, while part of the same book and the same chapter (or even the same section of a chapter) are published individually. The beginning also should have a hook or lead—an enticing first sentence that makes the reader want to continue reading.

Blogging a book and writing a book differ primarily in the fact that each post you publish must function as a stand-alone unit. You can link to earlier material you have published so your readers know what has come before, but a person reading one particular post may not have read previous posts. They may "pick up" your book at any point. In fact, a keyword search may point them to your blog at whatever page seems most pertinent to that search engine. For example, if someone searched for "why blog a book" on Google's search engine, they might find only this blog post of mine: "Why Blog a Book? You and Your Blog Might Get Discovered! (Part 9)." If they clicked on the link they would find themselves at part nine of a ten-part series of posts at the *How to Blog a Book* blog. They would, of course, have the option of clicking forward or back, turning the pages, if you will, of my blogged book, to read the other posts on the topic.

Therefore, as you write your posts, first write them as complete entities. Then, provide links to any other previously written posts that might be pertinent to the material you cover. Additionally, create a flow from one post to the next to keep your readers turning pages—reading from one day to the next. Do this by teasing them on. You might, for instance, say, "Tomorrow I'll tell you all about how to write a blog post," or "In my next post, I'll explain how to schedule your posts so you don't have to write a post every day." This entices your readers to come back for more.

When appropriate, you will want to add the words "In yesterday's post I mentioned …" or "In my last post …" and then add whatever you wrote about yesterday. Don't forget to also create a link (a.k.a. a hyperlink) to the previous post with some of those words. This allows readers to flip the pages easily.

In the same way, if you mention a term you defined ten posts back, provide a link to that post. If you discussed an important concept, create a link back to it. This provides continuity within your blogged book, which does not have an index or glossary. You could, I suppose, add a blog page with a glossary, but it's better to keep your readers clicking through to pages in your book.

Know that as you continue writing in this manner you create transition sentences at the beginning and the end of each post that you may or may not want in a printed or digital book. Don't worry about that now. You need these sentences for the blogged version of your book. Edit them out, if necessary, when you are getting ready to produce a different version of your book.

Using this basic post format, you now can begin writing. Start with your introduction or just jump right into chapter one. You can use the introduction in the "About This Blog" page if it works better there. In either case, chunk your book down to post-sized bits and keep them individualized but flowing one into the next.

If you want to allow readers to go back to "page one" of your book, or the first post, so they can read from the beginning, create a page with a link to your first post. That's what I did on the *How to Blog a Book* blog; I called it "Page One."

BE CONVERSATIONAL

Even if you are blogging a book on a technical subject or on a scholarly topic, approach writing your book in a conversational manner. Most people who read blogs expect the author to "talk to them" informally.

However, if you feel you must maintain a professional tone, then by all means choose that as the writing style of your blogged book. Only you know best what writing style will most effectively communicate your message.

Actually, your readers know best. You can ask them what they think or what they like. Try polling or surveying them. (You can add a poll plugin to your blog easily, like WP-Polls, Social Polls by Opinion Stage, or Total Poll by WordPress Poll, or create a free survey with www.SurveyMonkey.com.) Just ask readers to give you feedback via the "comments" function. At the end of a post ask: "Would you prefer that this blog be written in a more conversational and less formal tone?" See what types of comments you get back. Or write one post in a conversational tone and another in a formal tone, and ask for feedback.

If you aren't getting readers, which means you have no one to poll or to ask for comments, change your style and see if you attract readers that way. Maybe you need to stop thinking so much about your blog being a book and simply blog for a while. You can get back to blogging your book later. Keep your book's table of contents in mind, but don't marry yourself to it. Allow yourself to write in a more free-flowing manner and see what happens. Or try including more keywords; this surely will attract more readers.

I had an interesting experience when I began editing this book. I had blogged it and then put the manuscript away for about six months after completing the book proposal. As I started editing and revising it I found myself quite taken with the voice I'd used. I really liked it! I found my blogging voice friendly and chatty, yet authoritative. It sounded and felt authentic and highly readable. Some of my other writing seems much more verbose and formal; this writing was to the point while remaining warm.

Thinking back, I hadn't consciously decided to do anything differently when I sat down to blog this book. I was just aware of the fact that I was writing short pieces and that I needed to get them done quickly.

In reality, the posts for *How to Blog a Book* were fit into and around the other work I was doing. I was working with my book-editing and coaching clients, writing monthly articles for a magazine, composing blog posts daily for one of my other blogs, and doing other jobs as well. In other words, I was busy and didn't have time to dawdle over these particular blog posts.

I had the same experience when I edited another short book of mine comprised of ten blog posts. The warm yet confident voice I used for that book seemed to come from somewhere deep inside me. I had a friend proofread that manuscript and give me feedback, and she also enjoyed the tone of the writing more than some of my other work.

So allow yourself some freedom with your blogged book. No one is looking over your shoulder. You are your only boss. You are the only one dictating how you write this book or even what to write each day. No one knows if you are sticking to your Chapter Summaries or List of Chapters. There is no right or wrong way to blog it or write it. Express yourself in an honest and authentic manner. Let your passion, your voice, and your authenticity shine through. Let your readers get to know the real you. You'll be surprised what happens when you do.

In fact, that's the difference between a successful blog and an unsuccessful one. Successful blogs have at their helms bloggers who write with passion and purpose, who feel inspired, and who every day show up as nothing less than their true selves with all their colors flying. Almost every blogger I interviewed who landed a book deal attributed his or her success to feeling passionate about the subject of the blog and being authentic while blogging. If you feel the need for inspiration, go read their blogs.

You'll be blogging long past the time you finish writing your book. If you ever find your passion, motivation, enthusiasm, or inspiration for blogging or for blogging your book waning, try these to revitalize.

- Read other blogs on your topic—and comment on them.
- Get involved in groups and forums on your subject.
- Read books on your topic.
- Set up Google Alerts on your topic or on additional keywords related to your topic, open the alerts, and read the pertinent posts.

- Ask some experts to write guest blog posts for you so you get a break.
- Take a brief blogging vacation. (Tell your readers you are, in fact, on vacation for two or three days.)
- Do research on your topic.
- Talk to other people who are interested in your topic or who are experts in your subject area.
- Explore the possibility of using multimedia on your blog—audio and video.
- Interview experts in your subject area and post the information or the interview; you can even post it as an audio clip, a podcast, or a video.
- Videotape yourself talking about your subject matter or about the process of blogging a book, and post this as a way to let your readers get to know you.

USE KEYWORDS IN YOUR POSTS

One of the most important things to do when you write copy for the Internet involves using keywords. Remember, keywords and keyword phrases are the words on your site that match search terms. Search terms are the words and phrases people looking for information on the Internet type into the search forms of search engines.

Here's an easy way to discover the keywords for your topic: Think about all the keywords you might use while writing about your book. What words or phrases, for instance, relate to your topic? Also, what keywords or phrases might people use to search for information on your topic? These are the keywords and keyword phrases you want to use over and over again.

As you do, they populate your blog, blogged book, and website. They then are found by spiders, bots, and crawlers, or the programs that harvest information for search engines. The more keywords and keyword phrases on your pages, the higher your blog, blogged book, or website climbs in search engine results pages (SERPs). Also, the more often you post new content to your site, the more likely that these visitors will show up to index what is there. This means that if you post often and use lots of targeted keywords and keyword phrases, your blog and blogged book will move up in the SERPs. Eventually it will gain the coveted top ten Google ranking; when you search for your top keyword or keyword phrase using Google's search engine, your blogged book will show up on the first page.

There is a lot more to SEO than this, but using keywords and keyword phrases well provides a solid start.

I want to caution you not to get fixated on the need to use keywords or try to build them into your blog posts as you write. Here's why: If you stay on topic, you naturally use keywords in all your blog posts. You won't be able to avoid it. However, if you focus on using keywords, your writing becomes stilted, and Google, for instance, may decide you are using "keyword spamming" techniques to raise your blog's ranking in SERPs. Keyword spamming is a technique by which you use many keywords related to your subject—as many as fifty—and pack them into your content regularly. Not only will Google and other search engines fault you for this, your readers will as well. It's best to choose ten to twenty keywords and use them when they fit organically into your writing.

Here's another reason to know your best keywords but to write naturally about your topic in a targeted and focused manner: Google constantly changes its algorithms and makes updates. You never know how that might affect your blog. I had one of my blogs "hit" by a Google update, and I had done nothing scammy or "wrong." My traffic dropped somewhat dramatically over about six months, and I had to hire an SEO specialist to help fix the problem and get me back in good graces with Google.

I rarely bother to look up keywords for my blog topics. I know what they are; if I look them up, I do so simply to see if there are any I might not have thought of. Then I write about my topics day in and day out, and those keywords come up over and over again without me thinking about them. They are inherent to my writing if I stay on topic.

Here's the thing about SEO: It really comes down to great content. You can search out the best keywords for your topic and fill your content with those words, but at a certain point the search engines discover what you are doing—and they don't like it. If you are on point when writing about your topic, you will write keyword-rich content without any extra effort on your part. And that content will be valuable, which is what Google and the other search engines—and your readers—want.

By simply being authentic and writing great content, your blog posts will search engine optimize themselves. You will write passionately about your topic, and your copy will naturally include the words that attract readers and search engines.

This becomes even more true when blogging a book. Since you cover one topic for a long period of time, your posts contain many keywords. You write in an authentic manner and with an authentic voice. You do so passionately and from a place of personal or soul purpose or with a mission. In the process, you produce great content with superb SEO. At some point while you're blogging your book, your book should get noticed by the search engines and your ranking will increase on the SERPs.

It's a good thing to know what keywords and keyword phrases are most searched for on your topic. Create a list. Hang it up by your computer screen. Then forget about it.

COMPARING KEYWORDS AND WEBSITE RANKING

I am by no means an expert on SEO or on evaluating competitive keywords; I know just a little. That said, maybe I know more than you. So let me tell you what I know.

One of the best free places to compare keywords is with Google's free Adwords Planner Tool. However, you must first set up an Adwords account—even if you don't plan on advertising with Google Adwords. You can find the "Google Adwords Keyword Planner" by typing those words into the Google search engine. Then plug your word or phrase into the tool, and it will tell you if it ranks low, medium, or high and even will suggest related terms. Other free keyword tools exist, and you can gain access to paid keyword tools if you want to make that investment. These might have more bells and whistles and offer additional information you may find useful.

Don't get too excited if your keywords prove to be most popular. You actually may not want to rely on the most-searched phrases because they probably already have sites or blogs that dominate them.

Instead you might try to make a dent in less-used keywords and keyword phrases. You'll stand a better chance of working your way up to a top ten ranking on SERPs.

You can find out who leads the SERPs with your keywords by simply doing a search with those terms in any search engine. The top ten websites listed will be those with the most keywords or keyword phrases. Put the term in quotation marks and search again and you will get more accurate search results. Then see who is in line ahead of you.

The WordPress SEO by Yoast plugin helps you determine if you've done a good job writing your post and headline as well as the descriptive copy used on Google and other sites. Keep in mind that you must supply the on-page SEO by writing targeted content; the plugin then outputs SEO-related information displayed in SERPs and Open Graph tags needed for social media sites. This plugin must be properly configured to work well.

Now that I have gotten in way over my head, I'm turning back to safe ground. Let's discuss how to schedule the writing of your blogged book—something I know a lot more about.

WRITING ON A SCHEDULE

When I suggest to aspiring authors, especially those in need of platform, that they create a blog, most tell me they don't want to blog. It's just one more thing to do. In fact, writing a blog post every day or several times a week represents an unwanted writing commitment with a scheduled writing time and number of pages (in this case *posts*) to produce each day. They don't want to do this even if it means they are writing a book and building platform.

Authors who publish books one post at a time in cyberspace are no longer *aspiring authors*. They are *actual authors,* or published writers. These authors write and publish regularly. Like most working authors, they write every day ... or *most* days. Or so it *seems*. Let me explain.

If you have other writing projects to attend to on a daily basis or you hold down a full-time job, your blogged book can end up feeling like extra work. It can seem difficult to fit in time to write daily posts. And many aspiring writers complain they don't have time to write.

Believe me, I know that writing daily or even weekly posts can be hard. I have four blogs to keep up with on a regular basis, two of which require two posts per week. I publish a post twice a week on the third blog and sporadically on the fourth, although I used to post weekly there as well. When I started the *How to Blog a Book* blog, I already had three blogs, and I actually didn't plan to write another one. The opportunity just presented itself, and I took it. I then had to keep up with the blog on a regular—meaning three or four times per week— basis until I completed blogging the book. And after I'd written the book, I still needed to publish regularly.

When it comes to blogging a book, it's easy for me to say, "Remember, you are writing a book. Every aspiring author wants to write his book. So make it a priority." In some cases, you'll still protest, "I just don't have time every day to write!" I understand completely.

I've got good news for you: Blogging a book offers a huge advantage over other ways to author a book—especially if you are short on time on a daily basis. First, you write short posts. Thus, you do not have to set aside a lot of time to write. It does not take long to compose 300 to 500 words each day. Edit your copy once. Post it in your blog and proofread it in the "preview" mode. Make the necessary changes, and then hit the "publish" button. (If you can make time to find a photo, super!) The whole process might take you an hour, unless you are a slow writer. You will have written one page of copy.

In this way, writing three to four posts a week, I wrote the core of this manuscript in five months. Blogging a book helps you commit to writing your book; it helps you commit to finding time to write your book. Commit to three posts a week minimum if you truly want to find time to write.

SCHEDULING YOUR BLOG POSTS TO PUBLISH LATER

If you feel you don't have time to commit to writing your book every day, here's another great advantage and a phenomenal feature of blogging a book: Most blogging software offers a way to write in advance and publish your posts on a schedule. This means you can sit down today, knock out three to five posts, and then schedule them to publish at a later date.

Voilà! It then looks like you've been writing three to five times during the week when actually you wrote for a few hours one day, scheduled your posts, and walked away from your blogged book until next week or next month.

For example, when I began blogging *How to Blog a Book*, I wanted to publish three to five posts each week. I would often write a post and publish it on Monday and then immediately write two more posts in advance and schedule them to publish on Wednesday and Friday. That way, I knew I'd have at least three posts published in the coming week. I still had the freedom to write on the other days if I found the time.

When I run the Write Nonfiction in November Challenge (a.k.a. National Nonfiction Writing Month or NaNoWriMo), scheduling posts is a necessity. I publish thirty consecutive posts in one month, and most years I'm on vacation during the Thanksgiving holiday. Plus, at the same time, I'm trying to keep up with three other blogs, client work, and miscellaneous projects, like writing books and promoting myself. (I used to have this challenge on a separate blog and had to keep up with five additional blogs!) I get as many posts as possible written, edited, and scheduled so the blog basically runs itself most of the month.

Scheduling your blog posts is simple. The function for scheduling posts in WordPress can be found just above the "publish" button. (In most other blogging software programs it's in about the same place.) Find the prompt that says, "Publish immediately" with the option to "edit." Click on "edit" to choose the time and date when you would like your post to publish. Then click on "okay" and "schedule." (Usually the "publish" button changes to "schedule" at this point. If it still says "publish," don't panic. You probably didn't click "okay.")

Now go to "Posts" and "All Posts." You'll see the list of all your published and scheduled posts. Notice that the status of the post you just scheduled appears as "scheduled" rather than "published." If you had just published it, the status would tell you how long ago you had published the post. If you published it several days ago, it would just say "published." You also can find scheduled posts in the "scheduled" category at the top of the "Posts" page.

KEEPING UP WITH YOUR BLOG WHEN USING THE SCHEDULING OPTION

As you've probably realized, scheduling your posts offers a definite advantage for the busy blogger or author. Now that you know how to schedule your blogged book's posts, however, you are at risk. You may walk away from your blogged book all week and pay no attention to what's going on there, such as how many readers have left comments. That's a definite disadvantage to scheduling your posts.

You want, therefore, to devote one day a week to actually writing a live post—one you write and publish right then and there. This keeps things fresh. It allows you to comment on what's going on in the moment, such as news events that might affect your topic, comments that have just come in, or events in your life. It ensures that your blogged book stays fresh and alive.

If you have a time-sensitive blogged book, you may not be able to use the scheduling option often or at all. It's nice to know it's there, though, should you need it. After all, we all need to go on vacation.

As I mentioned, I tend to schedule a few posts each week and then write a few live posts. Actually, in the first three months of blogging *How to Blog a Book* (February through April), I wrote almost all the blogs live. That explains the long gaps between some posts. If you read my other blog *Write Nonfiction NOW!*, you may have noticed that on some days the posts don't show up until really late in the day—especially if you live on the East Coast. That's because I may have had such a busy day that I didn't get around to writing my post until the evening. For many years I wrote every one of those posts live, and I published three days a week. (For the first eleven months, I wrote five days a week.) You can avoid these kinds of issues by using the scheduling function and writing ahead in conjunction with writing live posts on the days you know you can schedule time to blog your book in real time.

If you don't choose to write a live post at some point during the week (besides the one you post just after your weekly writing period), be sure to show up and check out what's happening in terms of comments. Hopefully, your readers find your posts interesting enough to actually comment on them. If so, reply to those comments in a timely manner. (I'll tell you more about how to interact with readers' comments later in this chapter.)

If you've used the scheduling option, you also want to check in each time a blog publishes so you can share it with all your social networking sites, like Facebook and Twitter. (More on this subject in chapter seven.) This task is very important and shouldn't be neglected. It represents one of the best ways to promote your blog and gain readers.

LINKING IN AND OUT

Everything you do that involves linking into or out of your blogged book helps SEO your blog. Google and other search engines like to see outgoing links to relevant and reputable websites just as much as they like to see links coming in to yours. This indicates your blog's or website's degree of popularity or authority. So, as you write your blog posts, consider providing links to resources you find on the Internet to help your SERP ranking.

Network with other bloggers who write about the same subject. You might be able to ask them to guest post for you, or you might do the same for them. Your bio or theirs will contain links to your sites. This is strong "link juice."

Another way to add links to your blogged book involves commenting on other blogs. Read what other bloggers write on your topic and leave comments. The comment box always offers you a way to provide a link back to your blogged book, usually by putting its website address in a response box along with your name and e-mail address. Additionally, this drives readers to your blogged book, which, in my mind, is as important as SERPs—or at least they go hand in hand.

In addition to linking in and out of your blogged book, consider linking within your own blog. (See "How to Compose Your Blog Posts" earlier in this chapter.) Creating a link that emphasizes the keywords of another blog post—yours or someone else's—is considered good form and a great strategy. These hyperlinks can lead to your own posts or to posts or pages on other sites.

What no longer works are "blog rolls," widgets consisting of long lists of recommended or favorite sites. Only use this strategy if you are featuring your own blogs or some sort of special resources, because most search engines don't recognize these links; thus, they don't help your SEO.

Generally, any way you can link in and out of your blogged book will help your ranking and bring in readers. So, link, link, link.

RESPONDING TO BLOG COMMENTS

When you publish a post of particular interest to your readers, you know immediately—or almost immediately. Typically they let you know what they think about what you have written, especially if you write about something with which they strongly disagree or agree.

It's a good idea to reply to comments and to do so promptly. This shows your readers you appreciate them and the time they have taken not only to read your blog but to tell you what they think of your posts. It also allows you to engage with them. In this way you encourage them to continue reading, to comment again in the future, and to tell their friends to read your blog as well.

Creating a dialogue with your blogged-book readers constitutes an important blogging activity. If you can get your readers "talking," or engaged, you can get valuable feedback on your book. That's what you want.

Many blog programs allow you to decide if anyone can post a comment or if you will moderate all comments. (As mentioned in chapter five, find this under the "Settings/Discussions" menu in WordPress.) There are also plugins, such as Akismet, that help get rid of spam comments. You should monitor the comments on your blogged book as well, which is another reason to stay on top of what's going on even if you are scheduling posts.

You reply to comments from within your blogging program's "Comment" menu. If you have chosen to moderate all comments, you can go to the "Comment" menu and accept or deny comments. Once you have accepted a comment, reply to it. At that point, you can ask commenters questions about your blog and its subject matter, and get more targeted feedback.

If you aren't getting comments, you might not have enough readers yet, or perhaps you are not striking a chord with the readers you have or structuring your posts to invite comments. Sometimes readers are just shy. It takes a few people commenting before others speak up. At www.VibrantNation.com, readers used to comment often on my blog posts, which I also posted at *Write Nonfiction NOW!* and *As the Spirit Moves Me*. However, I get few comments at *Write Nonfiction NOW!* and *As the Spirit Moves Me*. (I've never gotten a huge number of comments at *How to Blog a Book* either.) I think this is because there are more readers at www.VibrantNation.com and the culture or environment on that website breeds comments. At my other blog, *My Son Can Dance*, I get a lot of comments simply because of the nature of the blog and the readers.

Be sure to include a call to action if you want reader engagement in posts. End your posts with a question, an unfinished thought, or a request. This encourages readers to leave a comment.

HOW TO CREATE CONTENT THAT GETS RANKED HIGHLY BY SEARCH ENGINES

It matters little if you are blogging a book or simply blogging: Content is king when it comes to getting traffic to your site. If you are trying to figure out how to create a blog with content that gets noticed, gets read, and moves you up in the SERPs, Google has some great advice. In fact, while Google uses certain algorithms to decide on search engine ranking, these are aimed at helping people find "high-quality" sites. That means they reduce the rankings of low-quality content and increase the rankings of high-quality content.

To help you produce high-quality content, why not use Google's standards? Doing so isn't hard. No, you can't use its algorithms, but Google suggests you ask yourself the following questions, which are posted on its website. I suggest you ask the ones that apply to each and every post you publish as you write your blogged book.

- Would you trust the information presented in this article?
- Is this article written by an expert or enthusiast who knows the topic well, or is it more shallow in nature?
- Does the site have duplicate, overlapping, or redundant articles on the same or similar topics with slightly different keyword

variations?

- Would you be comfortable giving your credit card information to this site?
- Does this article have spelling, stylistic, or factual errors?
- Are the topics driven by genuine interests of readers of the site, or does the site generate content by attempting to guess what might rank well in search engines?
- Does the article provide original content or information, original reporting, original research, or original analysis?
- Does the page provide substantial value when compared to other pages in search results?
- How much quality control is done on content?
- Does the article describe both sides of a story?
- Is the site a recognized authority on its topic?
- Is the content mass-produced by or outsourced to a large number of creators, or spread across a large network of sites, so that individual pages or sites don't get as much attention or care?
- Was the article edited well, or does it appear sloppy or hastily produced?
- For a health-related query, would you trust information from this site?
- Would you recognize this site as an authoritative source when mentioned by name?
- Does this article provide a complete or comprehensive description of the topic?
- Does this article contain insightful analysis or interesting information that is beyond obvious?
- Is this the sort of page you'd want to bookmark, share with a friend, or recommend?
- Does this article have an excessive amount of ads that distract from or interfere with the main content?
- Would you expect to see this article in a printed magazine, encyclopedia, or book?
- Are the articles short, unsubstantial, or otherwise lacking in helpful specifics?

- Are the pages produced with great care and attention to detail vs. less attention to detail?
- Would users complain when they see pages from this site?

If we are going to rely on Google to tell us how to get our blogged books noticed by search engines—which makes it easier for them to be found by readers—I'd also note that a time existed when a 150-word post was enough to be attractive to this search engine. Those days have passed. A post that gets noticed by Google now must have double that word count. No more writing lots of really short posts in an attempt to move up in the SERPs. You must have a more substantial amount of content in your blog or blogged book's posts.

ARE BLOGS AND BLOGGED BOOKS PROTECTED BY COPYRIGHT LAWS?

I frequently get asked a lot of legal questions, such as "If someone blogs a book—actually composes it in the form of blog posts they publish on the Internet—do they need to worry about copyright issues?" Well, I am not an attorney—let alone an intellectual property attorney—so I turn to credible, publicly available copyright materials to get started. But if I'm not sure about something I've read from that credible source, I consult intellectual property attorneys who can counsel me about the parts I do not understand.

Some of the credible, publicly available materials every blogger should read include the following from the U.S. Copyright Office. These publications are written for non-lawyers (but again, if they still seem difficult to understand, consult a qualified attorney).

- Circular 1 – Copyright Basics: http://copyright.gov/circs/circ01.pdf
- Circular 66 – Copyright of Online Works: http://copyright.gov/circs/circ66.pdf
- Circular 3 – Copyright Notice: http://copyright.gov/circs/circ03.pdf
- Factsheet – Registering a Copyright: http://copyright.gov/fls/sl35.pdf

I asked Gary K. Marshall and Robert Pimm, two intellectual property attorneys, to weigh in on whether bloggers should worry about copyright issues. Both agreed that bloggers should have a thorough understanding of their rights and should assert their rights effectively under copyright law.

Marshall noted, "Each word is protected by copyright as soon as it is 'fixed in any tangible medium of expression, now known or later developed, from which they can be perceived, reproduced, or otherwise communicated, either directly or with the aid of a machine or device.' So as soon as the word is stored in your computer or written on a page it is protected by copyright."

Also, despite some layman suggestions, Marshall explained that printing out your work serves no legal purpose when it comes to claiming copyright ownership, nor does the so-called "Poor-man's Copyright," putting your work in an envelope and mailing it to yourself.

A blogger's most effective step is to formally register her blog postings at the U.S. Copyright Office. The fee to file a paper registration form is currently $65; the online fee is $35. Copyright registration has two big advantages. If you register the work within three months of first publication then you can sue for statutory damages of up to $150,000 per infringement—and you may also get an award of attorney's fees, among other benefits.

"Let's say someone copies one of your articles. How are you damaged? You are out maybe a license fee of a few hundred dollars. It could easily cost you over $100,000 to sue them. If you have not registered your work, there is little you can do to stop them that makes sense to do. You would not want to spend $100,000 to collect $300. If you have registered the work before they infringed, you can sue for the statutory damages up to $150,000 and for attorney's fees, which as I said could be over $100,000," explained Marshall.

"Realistically, most writers do not want to sue; they just want to stop the other person from using their work," he continued. "If you have registered your work, you can almost always get them to stop when you write them a letter pointing out the high judgment they would face if they continue to infringe."

Pimm added, "The frequency of registration is open to debate; nevertheless, it is *strongly* recommended that registration be made at least quarterly (every three months) from the date of first publication."

"If you get in the habit of every three months registering the copyright in the works you have created in the last three months, you are probably protected," Marshall explained. "If that is too much, registering once a year will still give you most of the protection you need." (Read Marshall's free "Copyright Basics" at marshallcomputer.com/resources.html for more on this topic.)

Keep in mind that the determination of what constitutes "published" online is not a simple black-and-white matter. For example, Pimm notes that in Circular 66, in a section titled "Determining If Your Work Is Published or Unpublished," the Copyright Office states:

> "The definition of 'publication' in the U.S. copyright law does not specifically address online transmission. As has been the long-standing practice, the Copyright Office asks the applicant, who knows the facts surrounding distribution of copies of a work, *to determine whether the work is published or not.*"

Thus, if you consider your work "published" because your blog postings are on the Internet, the authors of the multi-volume legal treatise *Perle, Williams & Fischer on Publishing Law* would agree.

> "One more relatively recent issue has been whether posting written material on the Internet constitutes publication. Due to the wide-spread dissemination of Internet postings, *it has become well accepted that such postings do constitute publication.*"

"However, the consequences of registering a work as unpublished instead of published can affect many issues, such as access to statutory damages," explains Pimm. He recommends registering your blog content as "published."

Here are the basic steps to protect copyright.

1. Use a prominent copyright notice on all materials posted, such as: "Copyright © 2014. Your Name. All Rights Reserved."
2. Register the copyright of your blog frequently (e.g., quarterly).
3. Include "Terms & Conditions" as part of your blog, and require guest bloggers to accept these terms and conditions *prior* to any postings. (If you don't understand "Terms & Conditions," consult a qualified attorney.)

Another question I frequently get asked is "Do bloggers, or those blogging books, need to worry about plagiarism?" In my experience, it's rare that blog content gets used without attribution, which means plagiarized, or "scraped." You'll commonly hear this response to the above question: "For a typical author, obscurity is a far greater threat than piracy." (This comment has been attributed to Tim O'Reilly of O'Reilly Media.)

Pimm answered this question by turning it on the blogger: "Plagiarism is a serious problem for someone offering themselves as an 'expert' or someone in academia, because stealing ideas and research and passing it off as your own without proper attribution is academic dishonesty. Ultimately this kind of dishonesty will undermine the blogger's credibility and reputation."

He also noted that "ideas" are not protectable under copyright law, "but passing off someone else's ideas as your own without proper attribution is plagiarism. Thus, when using research assistants, bloggers should have them sign an agreement that includes language where the assistant obligates himself or herself not to plagiarize. This can help to reduce those situations where a blogger using an assistant is accused of plagiarism when they had no idea the assistant was engaging in such practices." You can use software like www.iThenticate.com to help identify plagiarism, especially if you run a lot of guest posts.

If you decide to start guest blogging on someone else's blog as a way to promote yourself, your blog, and your blogged book, it's important to understand the rights you might be giving away in the process. Pimm suggests that before you agree to publish a post or an excerpt of your blogged book on another blogger's site, you should do the following.

1. Read, review, and understand the other blog's Terms & Conditions in case they are claiming ownership of your blog posting.
2. If you already have a publishing contract, read, review, and understand the terms and conditions of your book's publishing agreement to ensure you even have the right to publish part of your book on another person's blog.
3. Read, review, and understand the agreement you have with your literary agent (if applicable) in case the agent is due to receive compensation from any publication and thus is entitled to a commission should you be compensated for your guest blog.

If you are serious about blogging, you should become familiar with the many legal issues related to blogging, blogging your book, and guest posting. Bloggers should also take the time necessary to learn about their legal rights and obligations under copyright law. The resources listed above are credible sources and are a great starting point. To repeat, I am not an attorney—so if you are uncomfortable with anything discussed in this section, the best course of action is to consult with a qualified attorney.

IT ALL COMES DOWN TO CONTENT

If you want to produce a blogged book people will read—one that generates traffic and gets the attention of a publisher sometime down the road (or gains you readers when you self-publish it), you must produce good content and lots of it. No other way exists.

Sure you need to promote that blog. Yes, a topic about which people want to read and a unique angle help considerably, especially if your blog has a lot of competition. Plus, you need to post often and consistently, use keywords, write with passion and authenticity, and have a market. But when it's all said and done, great content draws readers. Period.

In a *Sioux City Journal* article posted on November 28, 2010, Tucker Max, a best-selling author and blogger, said, "Content is 90 percent of any good blog. The 10 percent that's left? That's fixable. Anybody can learn good marketing or good design. But good content is most important."

Max's writing career started after law school, when he began detailing the events of his life—or, more specifically, his nightlife—to his friends via e-mail. "I had to write e-mails, and I realized you can't bull---- your friends. You can't waste their time. So I had to write something that somebody else cares about. That's how I learned how to write."

Those e-mails led to a blog about a single guy's exploits with women and then to the book *I Hope They Serve Beer in Hell*, which became a huge bestseller. Though a single guy's exploits with women may not seem like a great topic choice to some, all that mattered was that he posted good content on his blog on a regular basis, did it with passion and authenticity, and connected with people who wanted to read it. He met Google's, or some other search engine's, criteria, and for these reasons his blog rose up the ranks. He developed platform (partly thanks to the fact that Miss Vermont sued him—the suit was covered by every major media network and newspaper—and MTV released a documentary on him). He got noticed. He got a book deal with Kensington Books in 2004. The movie version of *I Hope They Serve Beer in Hell* came out in 2009, and his second book, *Assholes Finish First*, came out in 2010. (As the saying goes, there's no such thing as bad publicity.)

What if, like Max, you've been blogging for a while and think there's a book in that blog? The next chapter teaches you how to "book" your blog.

CHAPTER 7

HOW TO BOOK A BLOG

Up until this point, this book has focused on how to blog a book—how to consciously evaluate a book idea for publication online and off, map out its content in post-sized pieces, and then write, publish, and promote it on the Internet using blog technology. To assist long-time bloggers interested in publishing a book, this chapter focuses on how to book a blog—how to repurpose your existing blog content into a manuscript you can publish in any number of ways.

The majority of bloggers who have landed book deals didn't set out to blog books; they simply blogged their way to book deals. Once they signed a publishing contract, they had to figure out how to re-purpose all those blog posts into a manuscript that would read like a book and not a blog.

That's a harder task than blogging a book from scratch. However, I believe there are more bloggers trying to figure out how to repur-pose existing blogged content into books than aspiring authors try-ing to figure out how to blog books. Why? Because bloggers churn out tons of content on a regular basis, and aspiring authors some-times struggle to write more than a few pages. That means many bloggers—possibly you—have an overabundance of previously writ-ten and published content they want to turn into e-books and print-ed books. In fact, your blog could prove a virtual gold mine of viable book content you've *already* written.

The New York Times reported in 2002 that 81 percent of the U.S. population feels they have a book in them and should write it. If that statistic holds true as of October 24, 2014, that means about 259 million people in the United States alone have a book in their head that they want to get out. However, only 2 percent of that population will complete a manuscript—as reported by www.AuthorHouse.com in 2002. Why? Because there's a big difference between having an idea for a book and actually writing the book.

Many aspiring authors feel overwhelmed by the details of writing a book or don't find time to complete a manuscript. Bloggers, on the other hand, churn out the makings of books regularly. Most of them just don't know they are doing so—or that they can plan consciously to do so. They just blog, writing and publishing post after post, without a plan to publish any of their content.

WHAT TYPE OF BOOK CAN YOU CREATE FROM YOUR BLOG?

You probably didn't consider the type of book you wanted to write when you started blogging because you didn't know you wanted to write a book. Or, if you did know you wanted to write a book one day, you may not have thought about the type of book your blog content would suit best. Now you face a ton of content you'd like to repurpose or reuse in a book and the large job of finding a new structure into which to place it.

When you begin this process, start with some idea of the type of book you will produce. Then you can find models—published titles—to study as you book your blog.

Most novelists don't think to write their books in post-sized bits on their blogs. They may serialize their books, which is different; it entails posting whole chapters. Obviously, if you have been sharing bits and pieces of a fictionalized story on your blog, you could produce a novel.

Now that you have some idea of what type of book you might produce, let's move on to the six steps necessary to book your blog.

STEP 1: CREATE A BUSINESS PLAN FOR YOUR BOOK

Just as with any book project, you must determine if your book idea is viable. It has to be marketable, which means it should possess a high likelihood of selling to the potential readers in your ideal market. These should be the same people who read your blog.

The first step in this process involves producing a business plan for your book. Apply the principles in chapter four to the process of booking a blog. Go through the proposal process by producing the sections of a book proposal.

Then take the time to evaluate this information to determine if your book idea can be improved in any way. (For more information on how to use this process, also known as The Author Training Process, to craft books that sell, read *The Author Training Manual*. It also contains information on producing a business plan for a self-published book, should you decide to take that path.) If necessary, re-angle your idea, retool the content to reach a bigger or more profitable market, revise your material to provide more benefit to your readers, or change whatever is necessary to create a book that will be unique and necessary in the category where it will be placed in the bookstore as well as in the market you plan to target.

STEP 2: PREPARE TO BOOK YOUR BLOG

You now need to complete the process outlined in chapter three but with a few slight variations.

- **CHOOSE A TOPIC:** Choose a book topic from the many you have written about on your blog. Keep in mind how the topic you choose affects you, your current blog, and your continued blogging efforts. You may decide to choose the overriding topic of your blog for the subject of your book. If you have a lot of content on this topic, you need to hone it into a more focused (and manageable) angle.
- **DECIDE WHY YOU WANT TO WRITE THIS BOOK:** Previously, you were happy as a blogger. Now you want to become an author.

Why? What will this new status provide? What do you hope to accomplish by publishing the book?

Maybe you would like to increase your expert status. Surely, a book will help you accomplish that goal. It's possible that you'd also like to increase your income. While most books don't provide huge sources of cash flow for authors, they are an income stream and might lead to additional income streams as well. They can help you build a business around your blog and allow you to become a *blogpreneur* with products and services based on your book and your expert status.

As with any endeavor, clarifying your purpose and goals helps you achieve them. Your book's purpose should dovetail with your own. However, take into consideration your readers' needs and desires so the manuscript you produce is focused on providing them with benefit. Knowing what you want to accomplish means you know the value you will provide to those who buy your book.

- **CREATE A TITLE FOR YOUR BOOK:** Your booked blog's title does not have to be the same as the title of your blog. You might find your book title in a blog post title that encompasses the spirit of the book, is central to the concept of the book, or that went viral. Or you can create the title from scratch based on your mind map and the content you want to include. As you create the business plan for your book, you might rework it after you have studied the market(s) and the competition.
- **HONE YOUR SUBJECT:** Do this with a pitch. Rework it later after you map out the content for your book and again after you create the business plan for your book (steps 2 and 5 of the booked-blog process).

STEP 3: MAP OUT THE CONTENT FOR YOUR BOOK

Although this step was included as preparation for blogging a book (chapter three), the process becomes a bit more complex when you book a blog. Therefore, it requires more attention—and a step of its own.

The biggest mistake I see bloggers make when they book their blogs is simply dumping a bunch of posts into a manuscript and turning it into a book with no previous planning. They don't outline a book or plan for the *best* book possible. They just say, "Hey! I've got some great content here. I'll turn it into a book." That process does not create a commercially marketable book—one that will sell (to a publisher or to readers)—unless you have such adoring fans that they will purchase just about anything you produce. Even in that instance, you likely will get reviews that say, "The book was exactly like the blog and not worth purchasing." You don't want that to happen.

If you choose to use some of the blog-to-book services out there, like www.Blurb.com or Blog2Print.com, it becomes impossible to edit your content. Don't go that route. Even if you use a service like www.FastPencil.com, where you can edit and add content, be sure you follow the steps in this section to ensure you turn out a truly viable book.

Let's assume you've been blogging for a while—maybe even a long while. You have a lot of posts through which to rummage. This can feel quite overwhelming, maybe as overwhelming as writing a book from scratch.

Let's break down the process into smaller pieces. As with any book project, begin by planning out the content. Stop looking at all the blog posts you've already written, and ask yourself some tough questions about the book you want to compile.

1. What topic do you want to write about?
2. If the topic is broad (e.g., dog training), what aspect of the topic will you focus on (e.g., humane dog-training techniques)?
3. What subtopics will you include (e.g., training with treats, training with voice commands, training off leash, etc.)?

It's a good idea to look at what other books have been written on your topic. Make sure your angle is unique. You want your book to be different from the other books already published so it will "fill a hole" on bookstore shelves. However, this exercise can be completed in greater detail later when you work on a competitive analysis as part of the business plan for your book (see step 4). I also discussed competitive analysis in chapter four.

With the basic foundation now in place, you can map out the full content of your book. I suggest doing so using a mind map. (See chapter three.) While mind mapping is useful for deciding on the content—the posts—for your blogged book's (or any book's) chapters, the process works for booking a blog as well.

Mind map your booked blog as if you have no content written already. Imagine the best book you could possibly write *from scratch*. Brainstorm the topics you would include in such a book. Once you have run out of topics, organize them into large topic areas, or chapters. Any smaller topics, or subtopics, could become chapter subheadings in your chapters.

Now type up a table of contents for your book based on the mind-mapping exercise. You don't need to assign titles to the chapters at this point, but you can; simply name them by subject area. Under each chapter, list all the subtopics you plan to cover in that chapter.

Next begins the hard work: Find the previously published blog content that fits the structure and content of the book you created. Piece together a booked-blog manuscript in much the same way you put together a puzzle. In the process, you will discover the content gaps, which you will later fill with new, unpublished content.

If you don't think you have a full content plan for your book after doing your mind map, or if you feel overwhelmed by the job of figuring out what blog content belongs in your book, in each chapter, and in what order, hire a blog-to-book coach, book coach, or consultant. (This is one of the areas for which I provide coaching.) An expert can see the big picture of your blog and of your book. For all you know, you have several books living in one blog!

STEP 4: SEARCH YOUR BLOG FOR RELEVANT EXISTING POSTS

Before you determine what new content you need, discover the "gold" hiding in your blog. These are your previously written and published posts that contain content relevant to the book you just outlined during the mind-mapping exercise. To find these, you don't need to read every post on your blog. There are better ways to excavate the valuable ore.

Mine Your Categories for Blog Content Gold

The first place to look for pertinent blog posts for your chapters is in your categories. If you have used them correctly, they should work like filing cabinets for all your content.

Begin by looking at the subjects you have listed for each chapter. Then see if you have a category that relates to that subject in any way. If so, open up the category and search for posts that fill the criteria of your chapter.

For example, if I was booking my blog *Write Nonfiction NOW!* and was searching for posts for a chapter on writing for publications, I might look in the "personal essays," "articles," "journalism," and "magazine articles" categories to find pertinent posts.

One chapter at a time, work through all related blog categories—or all your categories, if necessary. As you find posts that relate to each chapter, copy and paste their content into a word processing document. If you know the order in which they will fall—what posts will come first, second, third, and so on—paste them into the document in that order. Knowing the structure of each chapter—and of the whole book—before you begin this process saves you a lot of time and work later.

Play Tag to Find Content for Your Booked Blog

Another way to find content for a booked blog involves playing tag … metaphorically speaking. Use the tag feature of your blog to search out relevant content for your book.

Tags are the search terms and phrases, otherwise known as keywords and keyword phrases, you have used in your posts. Hopefully, you have "tagged" your posts prior to publishing them. This is done in a small box on the page where you write your posts; in it you add a few tags to help search engines, and those using your site's search function, find posts by keyword search. If you have done this with each post, you should have a blog index of sorts. (If you have not done this, go back and do it for each post … please! It is a huge factor in making your blog search-engine friendly.) This index comes in handy now.

Here's how you do this if you are using a WordPress blog platform. (If you are using a different platform, it likely works in a similar fashion.)

1. Go to "tags" in WordPress menus. (It's under "Posts.")
2. In the upper-right corner, find the search box. Type in a search term that relates to one of your chapters. For example, if I were booking a blog about scenic design, I might have a chapter on models. For that chapter I could search for the term "models." For the chapter on drafting, I could search for the term "drafting." Once you have entered your search term into the box, hit "Search Tags."
3. Once the list is populated, you will see a number in the far-right corner of the list that tells you how many posts you've written that have that particular tag attached to them. Click on that number, and a new list will populate—a list of all those posts!
4. Click on each post.
5. Copy and paste the relevant posts into your manuscript.

Pretty simple, huh?

Find Content Using Your Blog's Search Engine

You can employ your site's search engine to help you find content for your booked blog. This old—and slow—search method requires putting keywords and keyword phrases into your blog's search engine (provided you have one). This brings up the blog posts most closely related in topic. You then search through them to see if you discover anything new you haven't found when looking through your categories or tags. Use this method alone if you have not used your categories or tags well.

Use a Program (or Programmer) to Extract Your Posts

If you are a Mac user, you can do what *LifeHacker* blogger and author Gina Trapani did. She used a Mac program called DEVONthink Pro. It creates a database of Web pages, plain notes, and word processing documents from your blog. You then can organize this data into a book outline. Using this program Trapani was able "to suck all five thousand of *Lifehacker*'s blog posts into its database immediately" as she worked on her book. Cool!

With that in mind, you might be able to find a coder, or computer programmer, to extract your blog posts into a database even if you aren't a Mac user. It's amazing what a good coder can do—and for very little money. Try placing a request on www.oDesk.com or www.Elance.com and see what you get back.

Some other options include using BlogBooker.com. This service will produce a Word document if you first export an XML document from your blog, which is easily done by going to "Tools," "Export," and then choosing "Posts." Then click on "Download Export File." You can choose posts by a particular time period or category prior to exporting the XML file. This service asks for a donation but has no set fee.

Or you can pay $250 and use BlogBookMaker.com for one week. This program requires that you first have your site validated (to prove you own the content) and then allows you to download posts into a Word file quite easily but only by category.

When you have finished extracting all those posts from your blog, you will have the makings of a manuscript. Don't, however, get too excited *yet*. You still have work ahead of you.

STEP 5: FILL IN CONTENT GAPS WITH NEW MATERIAL

Now that you have determined how much pre-existing content fits into your book plan, or structure, you easily should see where gaps remain.

If you couldn't find posts to fill specific chapters or to cover particular subtopics within chapters, begin writing.

There are two reasons you might, however, want to wait until you start editing your book to fill in these content gaps with new material. As you edit and revise your existing manuscript, you will find yourself in the flow of the book. This makes it much easier to write new material that fits well within the structure or in a chapter. If you write the new content now, you might have to further revise that new material later.

Also, the next step in the booked-blog process may cause you to re-angle, revise, or change any number of aspects of the book project you just created. It behooves you, therefore, to wait until you are sure the book you have outlined and the content you have compiled truly represent the best, most unique, and most marketable book you can produce from your blog.

STEP 6: EDIT AND REVISE YOUR BLOGGED-BOOK MANUSCRIPT

At this point, you have a number of posts that create the framework of a book and either new content you've added or that you plan to write. That's a great start! You are close to completing the first draft of your book, especially if you created a detailed outline, or table of contents, and placed your posts into your book structure in a reasonable order. If you didn't do that, you still have a lot of work ahead.

A good draft flows easily from chapter to chapter, section to section, paragraph to paragraph. What you have compiled does not do that ... yet. The reason is simple: The posts you previously wrote, while well written and published, were meant as stand alone pieces of work. You now have to create flow. You have to write in the spaces that exist between them. You have to compose transitions that create the illusion that all that content was written at the same time and belongs together.

In fact, the posts do belong together. The subjects all can be woven together, but that takes some creativity. So let's talk about the revision and editing process for a booked blog.

The first part of the process entails reading your manuscript. As you do so, look for ways to improve your blog posts and to create that flow between the posts. (Those who blog books have to do this as well.) This can involve:

- removing excessive use of lists.
- adding transitions.
- removing active links (for print books).
- removing mention of previous posts or next posts.
- editing out redundancies or any repetition.
- adding missing information.
- answering questions you feel you left unanswered.
- addressing readers' comments and questions.
- incorporating readers' comments and anecdotes.
- checking your grammar and spelling.
- removing blog titles and choosing the ones that work as subtitles.
- and more …

When you finish this process, hopefully you have a complete manuscript—the first draft of your booked blog. You may need to read and revise again, especially the new content you added. While your posts were edited previously, the new content has not received as much editorial attention.

With that job done, it's time to hire a professional book editor. Do not skip this step. Please. If you do, you doom your book. This is true whether you plan on traditional publishing or self-publishing, but it is essential for those who plan on taking the indie route.

Congratulations! You've booked your blog … or produced a finished manuscript from your previously published blogged content. Now, whether you blogged a book or booked a blog, it's time to turn your attention to promoting both your blog and your book.

CHAPTER 8

DRIVING TRAFFIC (READERS) TO YOUR BLOG

Let's assume that you've written your first blog post. Maybe you composed an introduction to your book and published it in one or more posts. You may even have scheduled two more parts of the introduction to post later the same week. How are you going to drive traffic—readers—to your blog to read the beginning of your book? In other words, how will you publicize or promote your blog as you start blogging your book and as time goes on?

Remember back in chapter four when we worked on your blogged book's business plan and I said you needed to think about promotion? Now we begin putting that promotion plan into motion.

Do you have your business hat on?

MAKING SURE THE WORLD KNOWS YOU'VE PUBLISHED IN CYBERSPACE

The first step toward promoting your blogged book involves "claiming" your blog with blog catalogs or aggregators, such as www.BlogCatalog. com. There are a few others, but BlogCatalog, an aggregator of more than one million blogs, currently is the largest. Here readers could find and subscribe to your blog via RSS feed and have new posts waiting for them to read in their browser automatically. The sites also give you the ability to track how many people have signed up for your RSS feed.

Blogs' standing and influence in the blogosphere also are rated or ranked by some of these sites. It's a complicated system involving a variety of factors, and it changes as the blogosphere changes. When you list your blogged book on BlogCatalog or any other such site, be sure to check the listing and set your categories to the most relevant for your content.

You'll want to have your blog posts automatically "pinged" to these sites as well. Now that you've claimed your blogs so they can be found, let's look at pinging next.

PING! YOUR BLOG HAS BEEN PUBLISHED!

Every time you write a blog post and hit publish, you want to be sure that post is pinged. A *ping* is a push mechanism by which a blog notifies a server that its content has been updated. An XML-RPC signal is a set of specifications and implementations that allow software running on disparate operating systems and in different environments to make procedure calls over the Internet. These signals are sent to one or more "ping servers." These then generate a list of blogs that have new content. That's a complicated way to say that when your blog post is pinged, a blog catalog or aggregator knows you have added new content. This ensures that people looking for blog posts or content on your subject matter on these sites can more easily find your blogged book.

In some cases, you have to manually ping your content or set up an account with these sites for this to happen. In most cases, however, this service is automated if you set up your blog correctly, or if you sign up with a blog catalog or aggregator. In WordPress it's an automated service.

Setting up your blogged book to ping out your posts is pretty simple—at least in WordPress. After you log into your WordPress blog, go to "Settings," then "Writing," then scroll to the bottom where it says "Update Services." You'll see this: "When you publish a new post, WordPress automatically notifies the following site update services.

For more about this, see Update Services on the Codex. Separate multiple service URLs with line breaks." Then you'll see a space to add site update services.

WordPress lists Ping-O-Matic's server (rpc.pingomatic.com) by default. It tends to be enough, but if you want to add others, you can.

Click on "Save Changes."

You also can use free and paid tools to help drive traffic to your site whether or not the functions used to alert update services have been disabled by your Web host.

Certain Web hosts, particularly free ones, disable the functions used to alert update services. If your Web host prevents pings, you should stop WordPress from attempting to ping and consider using tools such as Feed Shark (Feedshark.Brainbliss.com) or Pingler (Pingler.com). I have not tried them, and, therefore, cannot recommend them. If you are providing your blog feed via Google's Feed-Burner (FeedBurner.Google.com), you can sign up for its PingShot service, both of which are free. Please be advised, however, that there has been talk for some time now that Google may discontinue Feed-Burner. Therefore, this option should not be your first, and your feed is best provided via an e-mail marketing system like www.AWeber.com or MailChimp.com.

Having a long list of sites to ping used to be important, but things change on the Internet constantly. For a while, you had to claim "authorship" with Google, for example. Then that need disappeared. Today, it's imperative to have an XML sitemap. Creating a sitemap helps search engines more easily crawl and categorize your site. (See chapter five.)

AUTHORS MUST BECOME SAVVY SOCIAL NETWORKERS

In addition to pinging your posts each time you publish them, you'll want to use social networks to get the word out about what you've written. This means using Twitter, Facebook, Google+, Pinterest, and even LinkedIn to let your "tweeple," friends, followers, and connections know you've written something informative, useful, or entertaining. It seems every day new networks are born. Explore them all.

If you aren't already involved in social networking, start now. Do not wait. And don't dismiss social networking as a waste of time. It serves as one of the most important and effective ways to promote your book, build author platform, and, ultimately, sell books. Also don't skimp; join several. Some people dismiss Google+, but it offers great Google ranking for almost everything you do there. Others don't want to get involved in Pinterest, yet users of this site buy more items from the links they click on than users of other sites; that means they could purchase your book if they find it via the photos you post there. Even if you aren't blogging about anything business related, consider your book a business and join LinkedIn anyway; then seek out like-minded people who might be interested in your book in the LinkedIn groups, which is where the real connecting happens on that site anyway.

If you insist on taking a minimalistic approach, though, choose from the fastest-growing and most used sites—and those you think your readers use. Look at recent statistics on these sites. Here's a rundown on how the major social networks rank by rate of growth as of mid-2014.[1]

1. Instagram
2. Tumblr
3. Pinterest

Here's some information on social networks based on demographics.[2]

Social Networks Used by US Internet Users, by Age, July 2014
% of respondents in each group

	14-17	18-34	35-54	Total
Facebook	63.7%	83.2%	74.1%	76.8%
YouTube	81.9%	77.6%	54.2%	66.4%
Twitter	31.0%	38.7%	16.0%	28.5%
Instagram	56.4%	37.2%	16.0%	28.5%
Google+	24.6%	25.0%	20.4%	22.7%
LinkedIn	1.5%	15.9%	20.0%	16.6%

1. Source: GlobalWebindex Q2 2014

2. Source: *eMarketer.* www.emarketer.com/Article/Snapchats-Audience-Teen-y/1011335.

How to Blog a Book

Snapchat	36.8%	21.2%	4.2%	14.2%
Tumblr	23.8%	15.6%	5.7%	11.5%
Vine	31.8%	15.5%	3.5%	11.1%
WhatsApp	8.0%	9.8%	4.0%	6.8%
Reddit	8.0%	8.5%	3.9%	6.2%
Flickr	3.6%	3.9%	6.9%	5.4%
Pinterest	3.6%	2.0%	0.6%	1.5%

Note: n=1,093 ages 14-54; use at least once a week
Source: NuVoodoo as cited in press release, Aug 28, 2014

Pinterest may prove most useful to you, because you can pin the photos you use in each blog post. This drives traffic to your site. As an author and blogger, though, you may find Instagram provides a following that moves with you to other social networks and your blog as well.

When you take into consideration active users and accounts, the most common U.S. social networks rank in this order.[3]

1. Facebook
2. LinkedIn
3. Google+
4. Instagram
5. Twitter
6. Tumblr

While Facebook is the most popular site in terms of number of users—at the time of this writing it had 1.23 billion—it comes in second behind Google+ for overall website traffic.

Based on how many people visit various social networking sites, which indicates potential readers of your site, they rank in this order.[4]

1. Facebook
2. Youtube
3. Google +
4. Twitter

3. www.statista.com/statistics/272014/global-social-networks-ranked-by-number-of-users.

4. www.statista.com/statistics/265773/market-share-of-the-most-popular-social-media-websites-in-the-us.

5. LinkedIn
6. Instagram
7. Pinterest
8. Tumblr

If you want to know how to use these networks, there are plenty of books to read and tons of information on the Internet you can access. Just search for "How to use Twitter" or "How to use Facebook," and you'll be up all night reading for a month. Look for books that have been published recently; social networking practices change almost daily. For a general overview and some practices that will hold up over time, you can try:

- *The Savvy Book Marketer's Guide to Successful Social Marketing* from Dana Lynn Smith's The Savvy Book Marketer series (SavvyBookMarketer.com)
- Jan Zimmerman and Doug Sahlin's *Social Media Marketing All-in-One for Dummies*
- Liana Evan's *Social Media Marketing: Strategies for Engaging in Facebook, Twitter and Other Social Media*—or any book in this Que series on social media marketing
- the resources offered by www.SocialMediaExaminer.com
- Mari Smith's *The New Relationship Marketing and Facebook Marketing: An Hour a Day*
- Frances Caballo's *Social Media Just for Writers*
- Mitch Meyerson's *Success Secrets of the Social Media Marketing Superstar*
- Ekaterina Walter's *The Power of Visual Storytelling*
- Peg Fitzpatrick's and Guy Kawasaki's *The Art of Social Media for Writers*

I'm sure many of you don't want to learn to use social networks. Neither do the majority of my clients. "It's a waste of time," they tell me. "It means I have less time for my writing."

Well, it can be a waste of time, especially if you don't do your social networking effectively or economically. I'm here to say it can, indeed, be that time suck many writers fear it will become. I'm also here to say it does not have to be a black hole and to emphatically repeat that social networking is a publicity *must* for any aspiring author. There are platforms to be built on social networks. You can build one there. Your blogged book is a start, but you must implement your publicity plan with social networking.

If you engage in social networking, these activities will help you.

- **CREATE A FAN BASE ON ANY SOCIAL NETWORK.** These fans and followers become a built-in potential readership for your work; they might later purchase your book. They also may circulate the information you post—the links to your blog posts, the date of your book release, the times and places you are speaking or teaching. This allows their followers to read your status updates and click on your links, which, in turn, increases the chance that new people might check you out, read your blog, subscribe to your newsletter, follow you, and purchase your book.
- **DEVELOP EXPERT STATUS.** Every time you participate in forums and groups, such as those on Facebook, Google+, or LinkedIn, or in any way post information about your topic, you demonstrate your expertise about your subject area and give other people in those groups, forums, and social networks a chance to notice this. They will look at your profile. They will click on the links you have provided and then possibly choose to subscribe to your blog, follow or connect with you on a social network, or in some way become fans.
- **INCREASE THE SEARCHABILITY OR DISCOVERABILITY OF YOUR NAME, YOUR BOOK, AND YOUR WEBSITE OR BLOG.** Each time you join a social network you create a profile. This profile creates a link that can be found in search engines and also may have a place to link back to your website or blog. This increases traffic to your blogged book. The profile also mentions your name, your book, and your website. This makes all of these more discoverable in search engines because the social networks already rank highly—more highly than your blogged book or website. Thus, when someone searches for your name, they will discover you somewhere—on a social network or on your website.

In these ways, social networking provides a superb way to build your platform.

TWEETING YOUR BLOGGED-BOOK POSTS TO TWITTER

Twitter is a social network that focuses on 140-character messages that answer the question "What are you doing?" Sometimes "tweeting," which is what you do when you post to Twitter, is called "microblogging" because it works much like blogging, only with a character limit. Once you post a tweet, other people can "retweet" it—send it along—to their "tweeple," or followers, thus creating a viral effect, or "reach," by exposing your update to many more people outside of your immediate group of followers.

It's easy and free to use Twitter. Creating an account takes just a few minutes. Complete your profile, upload a photo, customize your site if you like, and write a short bio. Link your account to your blog website by including the URL in your bio.

Add a social media sharing tool to your blog so your readers easily can tweet your posts on Twitter.

You also can add plugins that help you easily or automatically publish your blog posts to Twitter. You can try WP to Twitter, Twitter News Feed, or Post to Twitter, for instance.

If you have added only a social bookmarking or sharing tool (plugin) to your blog and not one that automatically shares the post to Twitter each time you publish a post, you can "view this post" and use the share button that appears at the bottom of the post to tweet it (share it on Twitter). These automatically shorten the URL and add the title of the post. You can add a message to go with the title if there are still characters left. (Remember, you get only 140.) Or you can copy and paste the short link of your post into your Twitter status update along with a message. A short link is a short version of the long URL of your blog post. At the top of the page where you create a post, you will find a tab that says "Get Short Link." It appears after you have published your post. Click on it, and the short link will pop up. You can also shorten the URL of your posts using Bitly.com.

Twitter has its own form of etiquette. You'll want to Google this or utilize some of the resources I mentioned earlier in this chapter to learn how to follow other people and what type of information to post. (I mentioned some earlier as well). There are legitimate ways to gain followers, one of which is following other people on Twitter; I don't recommend get-followers-fast schemes. Providing a lot of good information, getting involved in conversations, and following people who seem interesting to you works best. As with blogging, providing good content is a strong strategy. So keep blogging and linking to the posts, as well as curating great content from other sources that pertains to your book's subject matter.

As a writer and blogger, you will gain the most followers by:

- staying on topic.
- following other writers and bloggers.
- following and actually conversing with other bloggers and writers interested in your topic.
- retweeting the information of other writers and bloggers.
- sharing information that is useful to other writers and bloggers.
- letting people know about your progress.
- supporting other writers and bloggers.
- following and connecting with experts on your topic.
- sharing content useful to experts on your topic.
- tweeting at least three times a day (more if possible) and at different times of the day.

SHARING YOUR BLOGGED-BOOK POSTS ON FACEBOOK

Some consider Facebook, another social network, to be just a place to keep up with friends and family, but many writers and entrepreneurs find it an extremely useful place to generate business. With this in mind, the savvy blogged-book promoter should share blog posts to Facebook regularly.

Once you have set up your free account by creating a profile, uploading a head shot and timeline art, and making sure you've included relevant links to your blogged book, you can begin manually upload-ing links to published posts if you like. You can do this in your status update bar where it asks you, "What's on your mind?" If this section was a blog post I wanted to share, I might first type, "Did you know that sharing your posts on Facebook is really important for authors of blogged books?" You then type in the Internet address of the link to your blog post (or even a shortened link), and Facebook automati-cally adds the post below your status update.

You may want to have a Facebook page, too. While Facebook pro-files are for people, pages are for businesses, products, etc. Technically, you can't market your books or services from your profile (although most authors do to some extent), but you can do this from your page. That's why it's important to have a page. Plus, having a page is more professional. You can think of it as your author page or your website hub. Don't wait long to start one; it's hard to drive readers to the page once they find your profile.

I must note that Facebook changes its look, policies, algorithms, and rules constantly. It has become more difficult to get content on pages noticed without paying for ads or promoted posts and pages. (That means that anything I write here or you read in books about this site could already be outdated.) Yet it continues to be an important so-cial networking site for authors and bloggers.

You can make your blog posts automatically publish to Facebook by registering for "Networked Blogs." You can find this "app" (appli-cation) by typing "Networked Blogs" into Facebook's search engine. When the Facebook page appears, click on "About." Then, click on the URL for the website under "Contact Info." You can then "Add Your Blog." Once you have the app, follow the instruction to register and verify your blog.

Next, go to your Facebook "Settings" and click on "Apps." Scroll down until you see "Networked Blogs." Click on "edit," and be sure that under "Visibility of App" you choose "Friends" or "Friends of Friends," and that you also allow the app to manage your pages, if you have a Facebook page.

Now go to the Networked Blogs site using the same link you used earlier, but this time log into your account. Find your blog on the left and click on its name. From here you can manage the syndication of your blog to your Facebook page or profile, or both.

Networked Blogs offers a way to tweet your posts to Twitter and to Facebook pages if you like.

All that said, it's best to get involved on Facebook personally rather than in an automated manner. Experts like Mari Smith, author of *Facebook Marketing: An Hour a Day*, advocate publishing updates with links to your blog posts manually even though it takes more time to do so. This ensures that a new change in Facebook practices does not affect you or your updates in any way.

Frances Caballo, author of *Social Media Just for Writers*, also does not recommend auto-posting to Facebook from your blog because your post becomes a "link post," which Facebook downgrades. "Link Posts are less likely to appear in your fans' news feeds. It's much better to use Facebook's scheduling feature within the status update box," she explains.

If you still want to use Networked Blogs, one option is to set the visibility to "Only Me"; when the app posts on your behalf, only you can see it. This can serve as a reminder to you to grab the link to your blog post and share it on Facebook.

OFFERING LINKS TO YOUR BLOGGED-BOOK POSTS ON LINKEDIN

Publicizing your blog posts on LinkedIn is a simple task. Once you have set up a free account—a much more detail-oriented task—you simply go to the "Home" tab and "Share an update." If you have created your profile and added a photo in the process, you will see your head shot on the left and the status update box next to it ready for your first entry. Before you hit the "share" button, notice that you have the option to choose if you will share the update with "Public," "Public + Twitter," or "Connections." This means you can share with two networks at once rather than one, if you like, or send the updates directly to those people in your LinkedIn network. To share on Twitter, you need to connect the two accounts; do this by going to "Privacy & Settings" and then clicking on "Profile." There you will see a link to "Manage your Twitter settings."

On LinkedIn you have the option of sharing links in your updates, so by all means, add the links to your recent blog posts. This is a great way to let people know you are blogging a book. If you are writing a book that has great information for professionals, LinkedIn is *the* place to share.

Since LinkedIn began providing its own blog platform for members, it took away users' ability to share a link to a blog on the profile page (unless this is your website address). You can, however, share your posts regularly by revising and repurposing them or copying and pasting them into LinkedIn's blog platform (about a week after they appear on your own blog); be sure to include a bio and links back to your site to drive traffic to your blog. I don't recommend using LinkedIn as your sole blogging platform as you blog your book. Instead, share related posts on this site and include a link to your own blog in your profile (and when you publish posts), where you house your blogged book. Or run excerpts from your blogged book as LinkedIn blog posts and include a note at the end that says, "To read the full post, click here." Then hyperlink to the full post on your site. You don't want to have your whole blogged book reside on another site, especially if you decide to use Amazon's Kindle Direct Publishing (KDP) Select program to produce an e-book. (More on this in chapter nine.)

You also can start a group in LinkedIn focused on your expertise. This provides a powerful way to use this social network. In your own group, you can syndicate your blog feed to post automatically on the discussion board. Members do not have this option. You can join groups and then post links to relevant blog posts in the discussion forum, but be sure to check the guidelines for the group before doing so. If this is not allowed, you might get kicked out of the group.

HOW TO BECOME A SAVVY NETWORKER

If you do not want to end up spending all day and all night socializing on the Internet, you must become a savvy networker. You can use all sorts of products, such as www.TweetDeck.com, Hootsuite. com, and www.SocialOomph.com, to help you consolidate your social networking activities. (New apps are released constantly.) These programs help you do things like watch all your social networks at once, send one status update to all your networks with one click, curate content from influencers in your subject area, and track the statistics on your status updates or links. They make your social networking more manageable. Join the networks and ask around to see what others use to help them keep their social networking streamlined. (Pay attention to status updates; sometimes these say what program the person used when he or she sent it.) Find out what the busiest social networkers are using to help them make their social networking time fast, easy, and efficient. If you ask them, they will be happy to tell you. Social networkers like to share. That's what it's all about—sharing great information.

What great information are you going to share? Your blogged-book posts, and anything else that relates to your blogged book, or to you as an author, that might attract people to read your blogged book. For example, you can share:

- related articles.
- others' blog posts on the topic.
- your writing progress.
- related breaking news.
- related book reviews.
- related movies and documentaries.
- details of trips you take to research your blogged book.
- quotations.
- suggestions to go read your blogged book.
- information about your upcoming speaking engagements.
- tips related to your topic.

Although I am constantly trying new services, those I currently use consistently to streamline my social networking and promote my blogs are HootSuite, TweetDeck, and SocialOomph. With HootSuite, I can shorten the link from one of my blogged-book posts, add it to a status update, and send this status update to several networks at once. I also can schedule this status update to go to all my social networks any time I like. So, if I've scheduled posts for a week, I can go to HootSuite, input all the links with a short message, and then schedule them for the days the posts will publish. I can even send them to Twitter, for example, more than once in one day—early and late, since people use Twitter at different times and someone coming on late might have missed my earlier update. I also can post and schedule all sorts of other messages to my social networks, such as those included in the list above. In this way, I automate my social networking.

If you want to track how many people follow your links after you've posted them, shorten them using Bitly, and then put these links into HootSuite. Otherwise HootSuite will shorten them for you. You can also publish the links directly to your social networks from Bitly. Bitly will then track how many people click on the link. SocialOomph also tracks click-through rates if you use their own link shortener.

TweetDeck lets you keep track of all your "tweeps"—friends, followers, and connections—in an organized manner. You can see if you've been mentioned or have received a direct message, and you can respond from this tool's interface. You can separate your favorite people to follow in columns or group them together into lists. I like using TweetDeck to curate content from those people I know, like, and trust. TweetDeck allows me to edit the tweets before I send them out and, in the process, to schedule them, if I like. I can curate and schedule posts for the whole week if I want.

SocialOomph has a variety of paid services from which to choose and allows you to manage several of your social networks from one platform. What I like best about this tool is that it gives me the ability to batch updates and to schedule them. I can create queues for different purposes, such as for a particular book, product, or event, and then batch status updates for that and turn on or off a queue as I like. I don't have to go to the site every day to manage it. It also offers you a way to manage your followers on several sites and to get keyword digests, which can prove useful.

Of course, if these services sound too overwhelming you can post status reports with your blog post links or any other information directly from each social networking site. As I mentioned earlier, I suggest doing this on Facebook anyway, since the rules of engagement change there so quickly.

For more information on tips and tools to help you manage your social networks, take a look at Frances Caballo's *Avoid Social Media*

Time Suck. And check out the previously mentioned resources to learn how to use additional social networks not covered in this book.

TAGGING BLOGGED-BOOK PAGES WITH SOCIAL BOOKMARKING

Social bookmarking involves using services like www.StumbleUpon. com, Digg.com, www.Reddit.com, and Delicious.com to "tag" content you find interesting or relevant. These sites suggest content based on users' preference, reading, or search history. You use the sites to tag online content, like your posts, as recommended resources. Unlike file sharing, users don't share the actual resources but just the "bookmarks" that reference them.

Here's how bookmarking works: After you write a post, you share the link on one of these services. Doing so requires that you set up an account. There are some who say using this type of social bookmarking can get your post indexed by Google faster than many other methods. However, others say social bookmarking only works well when you have a group of people who work together to add each other's blog posts and rate them (so you aren't adding your own content). You can try it both ways—on your own and with a group of blogging friends willing to help with the social bookmarking task.

Or you can simply hope your readers go to the trouble of adding your posts to these sites. You also can ask them to do so. Be sure your sharing tool offers bookmarking sites.

USING VIDEO TO DRIVE TRAFFIC TO YOUR BLOGGED BOOK

Another increasingly popular way to drive traffic to blogs involves video. At the time of this writing, statistics on the YouTube site stated that more than one billion unique users visit the site each month and over six billion hours of video are watched each month on YouTube—almost an hour for every person on Earth. Additionally, one hundred hours of video are uploaded to YouTube every minute. YouTube videos have become an ever-more popular form of Internet information and entertainment, and bloggers and book bloggers can and should use these videos to drive traffic to their sites.

Since YouTube constitutes the third most-popular website on the Internet today, you want to have a presence there. If you have a YouTube channel, you can post videos related to your blog to YouTube. You can share this link via your social networks and, if you've included a link to your blog somewhere in the video description, viewers can find your blogged book. Now, YouTube even offers a "Call to Action" tab, and you can add a link to your blog here. Also, be sure to add these videos in your blogged-book posts. (All blogging software has a function whereby you can add video right into your blog posts.)

These days, most computers, especially laptops, have video capability, and digital video cameras are pretty inexpensive and easy to use. Plus, your cell phone likely has video capacity as well. Without going into great detail, let me just say that once you have figured out how to videotape yourself, you can upload that video to YouTube. The videos do not have to be perfect. In fact, sometimes it's the imperfect videos that get the most views or go viral.

You can edit your videos. Your computer might even have the tools already, such a Windows Movie Maker (PC) or iMovie (Mac).

To use YouTube, here's what you do: Create an account. Then sign in. Upload what you have already recorded either on your computer or with your webcam. If you don't like the quality of your videos, re-shoot using different lighting or a microphone.

What can you record? Any of the following.

- a blog post
- information about your blog
- your mission statement
- the benefits of reading your blogged book
- tips or tools from your blogged book
- a book trailer
- a report on your writing or blogging process

Be creative and have fun. Record whatever you think might be fun for you to talk about or interesting for viewers to watch and hear. Who knows? Maybe your video will go viral. And by all means, share it wherever you can … on all your social networks! You might just have a lot of your friends on Facebook or "tweeple" on Twitter share your video!

USING ARTICLE MARKETING AND GUEST BLOGGING TO DRIVE TRAFFIC TO YOUR BLOGGED BOOK

While I encourage you to publish articles related to your blogged book in traditional print publications—magazines and newspapers certainly carry a lot of clout—when it comes to driving traffic to your blogged book, an easy and effective way to start building your platform involves writing and publishing articles for online publications. Many print publications have online versions that offer different content, but e-zines, newsletters, and magazines that publish only on the Internet often look for free content to fill their pages. Other bloggers, too, look for guest posts to fill their blogs.

It's easy enough to do a Google or Yahoo search for e-zines and blogs on the subject of your blogged book and then to submit articles to those you find. You even can submit excerpts from your chapters—blog posts grouped together to form an article. This provides you with a source of articles you don't have to write from scratch, and the editor or blogger might allow you to mention that they are excerpts, which promote your book further. Targeted e-zines and blogs provide your best promotional article tool online, because they have a built-in audience interested in your subject.

You can submit articles to e-zines for free; however, doing so can be quite time-consuming if you have a large number of articles. Therefore, in addition to submitting to specific e-zines that hit your target market, you can submit your work to an article directory. Directories provide free content to hundreds of different e-zines and bloggers looking for articles to fill their pages. In addition, anyone who chooses to publish your article is required to include a "resource box" with your bio and information that directs readers to your website or blog, or that mentions your blogged book.

There are numerous e-zine directories online. You can do a search for them and easily begin submitting articles. Most offer a free service to writers. The largest and most popular is EzineArticles.com. Each e-zine or directory has its own guidelines on article length, resource boxes, bios, and such, and none of them pay you for your content. Jeff Herring, the expert on using article marketing, claims that although the traffic he receives from EzineArticles has diminished in recent years, it still provides him with a valuable source of highly qualified free traffic.

The easiest and least time-consuming method for getting your articles in the most e-zines involves paying for an article distribution service, such as www.Isnare.com. For a nominal fee, these companies allow you to submit your article; then they turn around and submit that article to other article directories and e-zines for you. In this manner, your articles or news releases get the most exposure and may end up in any number of e-zines. Over the years, the return on this investment has decreased, however. Many such services have gone out of business, including most of the better ones. If you have the time, it's better to submit to a few e-zine directories and to certain blogs on your own.

Always put the resource box provided in an e-zine article to good use. Direct readers of your article back to your blogged book with a call to action. Don't make this about you but about something valuable you offer the reader, such as their next "success step." With this type of focus, you can create a unique way to get them to purchase your book, visit your website, sign up for your mailing list, and more.

One note of caution: In the last few years, Google cracked down on something called "duplicate content," which caused some concern in the world of e-zine article marketing. When Google spots duplicate content on a blog or website, it can lower the site's ranking. To avoid this problem, the best rule of thumb is to make sure the article or blog post on your website or blog contains 20 percent different content from the article you post in a directory or vice versa. Also, to avoid any problems with the e-zine directories or distributors, always write under the same name and have a similar bio. You can add PubSubHubbub, a WordPress plugin, to your blog, which puts a time stamp on each post to show Google when your post was published. This distinguishes your blog post from your e-zine articles if they are similar.

The last few Google updates have caused many people to shy away from article marketing in general, yet I see many experts still mentioning it as a good way to drive traffic to a blog. If this concerns you, try guest posting instead. This remains one of my favorite ways to drive traffic to my sites.

To become a guest blogger, locate successful, high-traffic sites in the same niche. These are the blogs you identified as complementary or competing blogs in chapter four. Get to know the blog and the blogger by reading the content on his or her site and commenting on it. Share the posts on your social networks. If you find that blogger sometimes features guest posts, find out how to propose one.

Guest blogging provides an effective promotion strategy. When your post appears on someone else's blog, you are introduced to his or her audience. Those people read your work, become acquainted with your expertise or viewpoint, and have a chance to click through (via a link in your bio) to your website and blog. The blogger may even let readers know where to find you on social networks. This makes guest blogging a fabulous way to increase your reach while, at the same time, getting endorsements from thought leaders in your subject area. The simple fact that these successful bloggers ran your post tells their readers they think you have something worthwhile to offer. (Then repay the favor, and you'll attract even more traffic by featuring their work on your blog.)

INCREASING TRAFFIC BY COMMENTING ON BLOGS

Another way to publicize your blogged book or blog involves commenting on other bloggers' posts. You know how you love it when readers leave comments on your blog posts and how excited you got the first time a reader actually left a comment? Now it's time to do the same for other bloggers. Let me explain why.

Each time you comment on someone else's blog, you create a link back to your blogged book—that is, if you leave your blogged book's Web address behind.

Don't ever opt for an anonymous comment. Always choose to have your website or blog address used in conjunction with your name, if possible. Then when your name appears with your comment, readers can click on it and the link will take them directly to your blog.

Not only do all these links increase traffic to your blogged book, they also increase your Google ranking. The more often you leave comments, the more chances you have of getting blog readers from other popular blogs to check out what you write. The more people who check out your blog, the higher your blog ranks in the SERPs. And the higher up it goes in the SERPs, the more easily it is found.

So search for and read blogs that have content that's related to your blog—and be sure to leave a comment.

If you found competing or complementary books, see if the authors of those books have blogs. Read their posts consistently and leave comments.

Do not spam these bloggers, however. By this, I mean don't simply leave links to your blog in the comment box. You must say something worthwhile; leave behind some useful information. Tell the blogger what great information he has provided, and then piggyback on his information with superb information of your own. The link to your blogged book will appear automatically if you opt to have your name link back to your blogged book.

I know that reading other blogs and commenting on them can be a time-consuming activity, and you'd rather be writing your blogged book. One way to handle this in a time-effective manner involves Google Alerts. If you have a Google account, type "Google Alerts" into the Google search engine and click on "create an alert." Fill out the form with whatever search terms apply to your blog. Then whenever someone writes about your topic, you will receive an alert and can click through the link to read the article or post. You also can subscribe to the blogs you find most relevant to your subject.

YOU NEED CONTENT ... SO GET WRITING!

The key to all social networking and promoting online comes down to the same point I made in chapter six: Content is king. That means that the ultimate way to drive people to your blog (or website) is to produce great copy consistently and often—and to share it. The more superb and useful your content, the more readers and traffic you will drive to your blog or website. If you produce good content and share it, you won't need to worry about Google's updates either, because it leans more and more toward ranking sites that provide great content. That's why this focus helps you rise in the SERPs. So it's time to get writing!

I see more and more bloggers offering great, free content on their blogs and social networking sites every day. The amount of content they produce amazes me. They could be writing books, and maybe they are. In any case, the content they produce offers added value to any and all who read their words. I often find myself clicking through to discover who these people are and what else they are writing.

With that in mind, I encourage you to offer great content that attracts readers—and agents and publishers. Offer it in your blogged book, in your social networking updates, in your e-zine articles, and in the comments you leave at other blog sites. Also offer free guest posts to other bloggers. However, while I feel strongly that content, indeed, is king, I would have to admit that many other things must be done to differentiate your writing from the other writers and bloggers out there—and every day more bloggers decide to enter the cyber publishing (and digital publishing) world.

How will you differentiate yourself among the million voices all striving to get the same attention and readership? How will you reach out to an audience already drowning in noise? Melissa Tamura in her blog *Zen College Life* at www.SmartBloggerz.com answered this question by saying, "Good content alone will not do the trick—there has to be something more than just hoping that people will read your blog entries." I've covered many of those ways in this book already. But keep that in mind as you write.

PROMOTING YOUR BLOGGED BOOK OFF-LINE

Don't forget about those off-line promotion activities I mentioned in chapter four when you were creating your business plan, such as public speaking, media appearances, newsletters, and print media. These offer great opportunities to drive traffic to your blogged book. They may seem counterintuitive, but they're not. You can garner blogged-book readers in a variety of places.

Do lots of public speaking. While many authors and writers balk at speaking, this remains the tried-and-true way to build platform and gain readers. Plus, you can send around a clipboard at each event with a sign-up sheet for your mailing list. Or use a short message service (SMS) whereby attendees text you their e-mail address. Offer them an incentive for subscribing to your blog and to your newsletter, such as a free gift of some sort.

Go to networking events and pass out your business card. Make sure the blog address is on the card. Introduce yourself as the author of your blogged book. This is a great conversation starter. Encourage your new connections to go read your blogged book.

Send out press releases to the media to let them know about your blogged book. Tie your subject into the news whenever possible. This provides a surefire way to get media attention. Radio and television interviews always lead to new readers (or book sales).

Subscribe to www.HelpAReporter.com or to Drew Gerber's Pitch-Rate.com, free services that let you know when reporters need expert sources for interviews. Then check these listings each time they arrive in your e-mail box, and respond to those queries that apply to you, your expertise, and your blogged book or its subject matter.

Write articles related to your topic and send them out to journals and magazines. It's true that fewer print media outlets exist today than in the past, but you may find some willing to publish an article or essay related to your blogged book. Don't worry about getting paid. Ask to have a byline and the link to your blog published instead.

Use traditional book marketing and promotion tools. You can find many of them in the following books.

- *1,001 Ways to Market Your Book: For Authors and Publishers* by John Kremer
- *Guerrilla Marketing for Writers: 100 No-Cost, Low-Cost Weapons for Selling Your Work* by Jay Conrad Levinson, Rick Frishman, Michael Larsen, and David L. Hancock
- *Guerrilla Publicity: Hundreds of Sure-Fire Tactics to Get Maximum*

Sales for Minimum Dollars by Jay Conrad Levinson, Rick Frishman, and Jill Lublin
- *The Frugal Book Promoter: How to Do What Your Publisher Won't* by Carolyn Howard-Johnson
- *Grassroots Marketing for Authors and Publishers* by Shel Horowitz
- *Red Hot Internet Publicity: An Insider's Guide to Marketing Your Book on the Internet* by Penny C. Sansevieri
- *Sell More Books! Book Marketing and Publishing for Low Profile and Debut Authors: Rethinking Book Publicity after the Digital Revolutions* by Steve and Cherie Miller
- *Sell Your Book Like Wildfire: The Writer's Guide to Marketing and Publicity* by Rob Eagar
- *How to Market a Book* by Joanna Penn
- *Author's Quick Guide to Marketing Your Book Online and Off* by Kristen Eckstein

Put on your thinking cap. Think outside the box again. Find ways to promote your blogged book everywhere possible, online and off. Don't miss an opportunity to tell someone about your book. Use that pitch you created in chapter four every chance you get. If you do this, you will find the number of unique visitors to your blogged book growing daily. And what could be better than that? Maybe finishing your blogged book and getting a book deal!

CHAPTER 9

I'VE FINISHED MY BLOGGED BOOK, NOW WHAT?

As you approach the end of your blogged-book manuscript and get ready to publish the last post, consider your next step. Hopefully, this decision has been handled for you along the way. While you were still blogging your book, you received a call or an e-mail from an agent or acquisitions editor who discovered your blogged book because of its popularity on the Internet and simply loved what you've written to date. The traffic you drove to your blogged book on a daily basis because of your promotional efforts provided necessary proof that a market exists for a printed book on your topic. If an agent contacted you, she asked for a proposal, offered to represent you and, subsequently, landed you a traditional publishing deal. If an acquisitions editor from a publishing house called, he asked for a proposal and then offered you a contract. In either case, you succeeded in accomplishing your goal. You wrote your book, published it, promoted it, and built enough platform at the same time to get discovered and published traditionally. You have both a blogged book and a traditionally printed book to show for it. Whoo-hoo!

DEAR AGENT OR EDITOR, DID YOU HAPPEN TO NOTICE MY BLOGGED BOOK?

What if your book did not get discovered by an agent or publisher as you blogged it, and it's now time to hit "publish" on that final post? Don't hang your head and assume you failed. You might feel disappointed, but your efforts have not been for naught. You have produced the first draft of a manuscript, which exists on the Internet. Anyone interested can sample your superb writing and well-honed and -executed concept.

Plus, you have built some amount of platform. If you have done all the things discussed in this book thus far, you should have unique visitors and page views to show for your efforts. (If you don't, you need to increase your promotional efforts.) You can feel proud of that as well—and you can and should share these facts with acquisitions editors and literary agents.

If you're a traditional publishing holdout—an aspiring author who does not want to self-publish a printed version of her blogged book—and this blogged-book "exercise" managed to get you to write your whole manuscript but didn't get you discovered—you have three things left to do: Write a fabulous query, write a phenomenal proposal, and approach a literary agent or a small or midsized publisher.

Literary agents work as writers' business partners. They represent you to publishing houses, or more accurately, to publishing houses' acquisitions editors (the ones responsible for finding new books to publish). They look out for your best interests when it comes to negotiating the publishing contract. A great agent also has your long-term career goals in mind. To find agents and discover what kind of submissions they want to receive, look in the annual edition of Writer's Digest's *Guide to Literary Agents* or *Writer's Market*, or in *Jeff Herman's Guide to Book Publishers, Editors, & Literary Agents*.

Most small and midsized publishers accept unagented work, meaning they will accept a proposal and ultimately a manuscript from authors not represented by literary agents, but large publishers (and some midsized publishers) will not. Some publishers have websites with guidelines. You can approach the small and midsized publishers on your own if you like; some agents will approach these for you, but many will not.

Here's the great news: You have already done the groundwork—created a business plan—that allows you to quickly begin submitting a book proposal to agents and publishers. If a traditional publishing deal remains your dream, begin writing a query letter and a book proposal immediately; by editing and polishing your business plan you will develop a great book proposal. In fact, if you are reading this chapter before that last blog post goes out into cyberspace, start composing these documents and sending them out now. Be proactive. No need to wait to be found. Help those agents and publishers along. You can send out your query letter at any point after you start blogging your book.

If you haven't yet written your proposal, go back to chapter four and take all the information you compiled during the proposal process, or the Author Training Process, and put a proposal together. The proposal contains not just the nine essential elements we used in the proposal process but also the complete list of the sixteen elements a publisher uses to determine whether your book fits their list of published books (and those they plan to publish in the future). The publisher will also gauge whether a market exists for the book and if they feel you are both the right person to write the book and the best person to become the company's business partner.

If you aren't sure what a proposal looks like or what format one should have, check out some of the great books on the market, like Michael Larsen's *How to Write a Book Proposal*, Jeff Herman and Deborah Levine Herman's *Write the Perfect Book Proposal*, and Sheree Bykofsky and Jennifer Basye Sander's *The Complete Idiot's Guide to Getting Published*. My book *The Author Training Manual* helps you accumulate the information necessary for a proposal. Plus, my e-book, *The Nonfiction Book Proposal Demystified: An Easy-Schmeazy Guide to Writing a Business Plan for Your Book*, provides all the information you need in a short format. Couple it with my proposal template, *The Easy-Schmeazy Book Proposal Template,* and you're ready to submit a proposal in no time flat. (The template is available at writenonfiction now.com/landing/easy-schmeasy-book-proposal-template.)

After you have put your book proposal together, have it professionally edited. The nonfiction book proposal represents the most important selling document you create. As the old adage goes, "You only have one chance to make a first impression." That holds true when pitching a book. Let a professional editor help you make the best first impression possible. Make every word count, and present an error-free document. Also, be sure the editor you choose knows what goes into a nonfiction book proposal; many do not. Don't use just any editor. You can find editors on LinkedIn, at writers conferences, in writers' clubs, through referrals from other authors, or even from agent referrals (ask their assistants).

Then write a great query letter and have this edited professionally as well. Again, make a good first impression! A query letter contains three things: a lead paragraph that entices an agent or publisher to read your manuscript, your pitch (which includes information about the length of your book and its benefits to readers as well as the special features you want to highlight), and why you are the perfect person to write the book. If you want to learn more about how to write a query letter, check out *How to Write Irresistible Query Letters* by Lisa Collier Cool, *Making the Perfect Pitch* by Katharine Sands, *The Writer's Digest Guide to Query Letters* by Wendy Burt-Thomas, or *How to Write Attention-Grabbing Query & Cover Letters* by John Wood.

Once the letter is flawless, send it to the agents you would like to have represent you or to the small or midsized publishers you feel are right for your book. Typically, the proposal does not go out with the query letter, although some agents or publishers may ask to see it along with a query letter. Again, check guidelines in *Guide to Literary Agents, Writer's Market, Jeff Herman's Guide to Book Publishers, Editors, & Literary Agents*, or the websites for each specific agent or publisher.

If your query gets a positive response, send your proposal as requested along with a cover letter. Then wait for an acceptance or a rejection. If you get a rejection, repeat the process. You can send more than one query at a time; a simultaneous submission is certainly allowed. (Note that some agents and publishers prefer not to receive multiple submissions.) Sometimes, however, it's best to wait and see what response you get to your query and proposal so you can make adjustments to both based on the feedback you receive—that is, of course, if you don't get an acceptance immediately.

Don't give up if you are rejected many times. Even the best authors received hundreds of rejection letters. I've heard this advice: When you get a rejection letter, just say, "Next." Or say, "I must have sent that query to the wrong address. Next time I'll send it to the right address."

WHAT YOU AND YOUR BLOG "NEED" TO LAND AN AGENT

One of the questions I am asked most often is "What are agents and acquisitions editors looking for in terms of blog stats and social networking numbers?" In other words, what type of platform must you build before an agent will seriously look at you and your blog? The answer varies significantly from agent to agent and from editor to editor (especially depending on the size of the publishing company for which they work).

I asked two agents who represent a fair number of bloggers for their input on this subject. According to Kate McKean, vice president and literary agent at Howard Morhaim Literary Agency, Inc., "The same things that make a writer in any form attractive to agents and editors make a blogger attractive: a strong voice, a well-thought-out project, a marketable project, and an engaged readership. The benefit bloggers have over an off-line writer is (hopefully!) a dedicated following already in place that can be tapped when the book hits the shelves."

To convince an agent or acquisitions editor your blog makes a good book idea, however, ensure your idea "makes sense both on- and off-line," recommends McKean. "Does the idea actually translate to print, or is it too ephemeral? Will it withstand the lengthy book-production timeline, or is it only fresh online in the moment? Agents and editors agree—any blog project must make undeniable sense as a book project, period."

When you write your query and proposal, do so just as if you were proposing a "normal" book. After all, you are an aspiring author and a writer. You also are a blogger, though. "Bloggers must share their metrics—their site traffic, social media stats, and/or significant press mentions or clippings. In terms of metrics, agents and editors want to see average monthly page views and average monthly unique visitors over time, preferably accounting for more than six months of data collecting," reports McKean. Reiterating similar information presented in this book, she adds, "Don't say 'hits.' Hits are meaningless."

Agent Ted Weinstein, founder of Ted Weinstein Literary Management, cautions bloggers not to get distracted by trying to reach a certain number of unique readers, page views, or followers. "An author who is eager won't wait until they cross some threshold of followers, and there isn't some arbitrary number which is a binary switch for an author's potential," he says.

Yet, he concludes that "tens of thousands of monthly visitors is okay; hundreds of thousands is better" for your blog. On Twitter, Instagram, and Tumblr, "tens of thousands minimum. Everything else—regular writing in *other* outlets, public speaking, etc.—is even better, but that's not specifically about blogging."

McKean explains that when agents and editors evaluate an author's platform, the necessary numbers vary by genre. "Thirty thousand average monthly unique visitors might be great for a lifestyle blog, but it's not much for a viral content/humor blog. And any one of these platform elements may be more important in one genre or another. A memoirist/blogger may do great on the speaking circuit but have low Instagram numbers because her demographic doesn't use Instagram. Agents and editors take all numbers and stats together and measure it against what's important to the audience of that particular project. There's no one magic number for any platform."

Basically, you can take all these numbers with a grain of salt and set about blogging a successful book or creating a popular blog. I didn't have tens of thousands of anything when I landed my book deal for *How to Blog a Book*. I did have five blogs at the time (with cumulatively more than tens of thousands of unique visitors). I also had a medium-sized social media platform and was a public speaker on my topic. I had a timely idea that worked online and off as a book as well as a growing readership.

If you are concerned that an agent or publisher won't want to represent you because you have blogged your book (rather than planning to book your blog), here's what McKean had to say: "I don't see the difference here, because I don't believe the reader would see the difference.

That's what matters most. If it makes a difference for the author in how she writes the content, and one way works better than the other, then she should go with what produces the best content, period. In either case, the publisher is going to require that some content be created or held back that is exclusive to the book, so whether that happens by design or by chance from the author's point of view, it doesn't matter."

FROM BLOGGER TO SELF-PUBLISHER

If you don't want to pursue a traditional publishing deal (or don't land one), consider alternative ways of getting your manuscript off the Internet and into some sort of printed version. As a blogger, you have self-published your book already (or a good bit of it) on the Internet. However, you can step up your game and begin self-publishing print books as well.

You might, for instance, produce a print-on-demand (POD) book from your manuscript. This is not so difficult to do and a fairly inexpensive option. With this type of self-published book, in many cases you can print as few as twenty books or none at all to start. As buyers purchase books, more copies are printed "on demand"—one at a time. Another option is offset printing, the "true self-publishing" route, which typically requires printing large quantities of books you might need to store in your garage.

Or you can take a more high-tech approach and turn your blogged book into an e-book. This constitutes a great option if you don't want to spend a lot of money and want to make your book available for the variety of e-readers on the market today. With e-books comprising a huge portion of book sales (approximately 30 percent of all book sales according to *Forbes* in February 2014), authors who don't make their books available on e-readers miss a great sales opportunity. Plus, this is the most inexpensive self-publishing option and allows you to get in on today's biggest publishing trend.

Of course, you can just leave your blogged book up as a completed blogged book. However, if it remains dormant for long, it will lose readership. People still will find it as they use search engines for particular terms and phrases, but it will fall in the SERPs if you don't add new content. If you choose this option, consider adding a new post once a week at a minimum.

If you leave the blog dormant as a sales page for a printed book or e-book as well, simply add copy occasionally to help drive buyers to the site. Again, it's better to keep adding content regularly (i.e., keep the blog alive) and drive traffic there for the purpose of increasing book sales.

TURNING YOUR BLOGGED BOOK INTO A POD BOOK

If you want to self-publish your blogged book as a printed book, you can choose several methods to do so. First, however, you must have a manuscript.

As I mentioned previously, the easiest way to blog a book and produce a manuscript entails writing your posts in Microsoft Word (or a similar program, such as Pages) and then copying and pasting them into your blogging software. If you have done this, you now have a complete manuscript. If you haven't, you need to copy and paste your blog posts into a document, which can prove quite a chore.

Even if you have created a manuscript, go back to your blog and look for information to add to it from reader comments and your replies. Also, if you planned to add fresh copy or features to your printed book, this is the time to do so—before you hand the manuscript over to your editor or book designer.

Once you have a manuscript composed of all your posts, divide your posts into chapters—if you didn't do this earlier. Then edit the chapters to make sure the posts flow together smoothly and read well. You don't want them to be choppy or to sound like a bunch of 300-word posts slapped together. At this point, these short posts need to read like sections in a longer chapter. Your post titles should appear like subheads. Edit out all references to previous posts or to what posts are coming next. Unless you are creating an e-book, remove all hyperlinks or fully write them out. (If you are creating an e-book, include "clickable" links.) Make sure you delete all references to "this blog" or "this blogged book" from your manuscript and instead make reference to a "book" since readers will read a printed book and not a blogged book. Check that you don't have too many lists or questions with answers as well; these are more appropriate on a blog than in a book.

Once you have edited the manuscript, send it to a professional editor for another round of polishing (or two or three). Do not skip this step or skimp here. Many self-published authors fail to have their manuscripts professionally edited and end up with books that do not meet the same quality standards as traditionally published books. Don't let your book fall into this category after all your hard work. It will not sell well if it is obviously self-published, and this fact will be evident in its lack of professional editing.

Hire both a developmental editor and a copyeditor or line editor. You may also want to hire a content editor. Developmental editors will check that everything in your book makes sense, flows, and that nothing is missing or misplaced. They may delete or move copy. They will point out redundancies and inconsistencies, and make suggestions on how you can improve your book. Content editors check your content to make sure it is correct: that the period clothing you describe is accurate, that the facts you mention are correct, that the dates that parallel news events related to your story line up. Copyeditors or line editors correct grammar, punctuation, and syntax and generally strengthen your sentence structure and overall writing. It's usually best to hire a developmental editor for the first round of editing and then a copyeditor or line editor for the second round; sometimes an editor will do more than one type of editing. The best editing jobs involve two or three rounds, sometimes more. You could have two rounds with a developmental editor to make sure you strengthen your book in general and then two rounds of line editing to ensure your writing is clean and strong. You could throw in a round of content editing as well.

Even great writers need great editors. Most writers are too close to their work to edit well themselves. Your book and you will appear unprofessional if the manuscript contains errors.

Also consider hiring an indexer; most nonfiction books benefit from an index, and it's best completed by a professional. You may want to have someone create a glossary for your book as well. Don't let your book fail because you skimped on these steps.

Last, but not least, hire a proofreader. Proofreaders provide a different skill than editors. They catch all the minor errors made during editing—a word not caught by the spell-checker, a second period left unnoticed among the many changes made, too many spaces between words, possibly even a stray comma that doesn't fit the style used throughout the book.

At this point, you need a book design. Simpler said than done—especially for writers. Do not design the book yourself unless you have professional design skills. Another distinction between many self-published books and their traditionally published counterparts can be found in design. Don't raise the self-published flag with unprofessional design. Instead, hire a professional book designer. Covers sell books.

Your book designer should know all about photo and art permissions and how to make stock photos look unique to your cover. Many POD publishers, usually subsidy or author services publishers like BookLocker, iUniverse, Xlibris, PublishAmerica, Author House, and Lulu, offer packages that include cover and interior design. These covers tend to look like they were produced on an assembly line. The more unique your cover and interior, the better. A professional designer will give you a design unlike anyone else's.

You can produce a POD book using a subsidy or author services press, which offer a variety of services to help you, like editing and design. Their editing services likely will be light copyediting or line editing; sometimes they provide developmental editing. If you use their design services you run the risk of other books having the exact same interior design or cover image or designs similar to yours. Most will publish your book under their imprint as well because they purchase the ISBN for you. This means the subsidy press's name will appear on the bound side, or spine, of the book. This also means you are not the publisher of record; they are. This is fine if:

- you don't plan on becoming your own publishing house and running a business as a book publisher—the true meaning of self-publishing.
- you want help and hand-holding every step of the way through the self-publishing process.
- you don't want to learn how to self-publish (you just want to get your book published).
- you don't want to hire editors, a designer, purchase an ISBN, etc.

- you don't want a book that is taken seriously by those who know something about publishing.
- you don't want a commercially viable book.

It's not fine if:

- you plan on self-publishing more than one book.
- you want to create a publishing company.
- you want to have all your books published under your imprint—your publishing company name—and have that name on the spine of the book.
- you want to learn how to do everything necessary to self-publish a book or hire the best people to help you.
- you don't mind hiring and managing editors and a designer, purchasing ISBNs, etc.
- you want a book that is taken seriously by those who know something about publishing.
- you want a commercially viable book.

If you fall into the latter category, contract the services that subsidy or author services presses offer on your own and then go directly to a POD printer, like Ingram Spark, BookBaby, or Amazon's CreateSpace, and have the book printed. (BookLocker allows you to use your own ISBN as well.) If you do the latter, you can decide on your own publishing company name (imprint) and have this printed on the spine. You become the publisher of record. Now you have truly self-published your book.

OTHER BLOG-TO-PRINT-BOOK OPTIONS

If you want to become a full-fledged self-publisher, you can go to an offset printer. These printers specialize in short-run book manufacturing, and they are by far the most economical option for printing (and offer the best quality, too). In this case, you have to actually order copies of your book, store them, and ship them out yourself (unless you opt for a distributor).

If you don't want to print one thousand books, or you need books quickly, there are printers who use other types of presses and will print short runs extremely fast; the price per book is higher but still affordable. You will have to ship the books to buyers or opt for a distributor. In some cases, these presses will distribute to Amazon for a fee.

Be sure to consult these great resources for all the things you need to produce and print your blogged book. There are many great books out there about how to self-publish, such as:

- *APE: Author, Publisher, Entrepreneur: How to Publish a Book* by Guy Kawasaki and Shawn Welch
- *Self-Publishing Boot Camp Guide for Authors: Step-by-Step to Publishing, Promoting and Selling Your Book in Print and Every Popular Ebook Format (3rd Edition)* by Carla King
- *Self-Publishing Books 101: A Step-by-Step Guide to Publishing Your Book in Multiple Formats* by Shelley Hitz and Heather Hart
- *Dan Poynter's Self-Publishing Manual: How to Write, Print, and Sell Your Own Book*
- *The Complete Guide to Self-Publishing: Everything You Need to Know to Write, Publish, Promote, and Sell Your Own Book* by Marilyn Ross and Sue Collier
- *The Indie Author Guide: Self-Publishing Strategies Anyone Can Use* by April L. Hamilton
- *Self-Publishing for Dummies* by Jason R. Rich
- *The Kindle Publishing Bible: How to Sell More Kindle Ebooks on Amazon* by Tom Corson-Knowles
- *The Fine Print of Self-Publishing, Fourth Edition: Everything You Need to Know About the Costs, Contracts, and Process of Self-Publishing* by Mark Levine

You might want to check out companies that convert your blog to a book without changing a thing, such as www.Blurb.com, BlogBooker.com, and Blog2Print.com. This is an option if you want your printed book to appear identical to your blogged book, though I don't recommend this if you want your book to read like an actual book or to sell commercially. If for some reason, however, that's what you desire, simply do a search on Google and you will find a variety of companies that offer blog-to-book services.

If you're looking for a way to directly import your blog post to a program that will produce an e-book or printed (POD) book for you, I recommend www.FastPencil.com. This platform allows you to import content easily straight from your blog or with an XML file, reformat posts into a book design using their automatic templates, upload a cover, and edit content. You even can invite in an editor. FastPencil also offers typical POD services, such as distribution and subsidy press services, which include editing and cover design. (Or, better yet, hire an editor or designer familiar with the site from the FastPencil marketplace—or bring in your own). Plus, this service provides e-book conversion services. Overall, this is the easiest tool for going from blog to book—print or digital.

Keep in mind that FastPencil operates as both a publishing service and distributor with associated accounts, sales fees, and per-book annual maintenance fees. You can pay $600 up front and $100 per publication for a Publisher account, which allows you to have your own imprint. That means you set up your own publishing company within FastPencil, paying the lesser amount each time you publish a book so your company name goes on the spine of your book rather than the FastPencil imprint. This makes you the publisher of record, not Fast-Pencil. Or you can use their author services. Here you choose to produce a DIY (do-it-yourself) print book under the FastPencil imprint for $249 or a DIY print and e-book under their imprint for $299. If you want assistance, you can purchase higher-priced author services packages, which I don't recommend. (I don't recommend using author services from most subsidy publishers.) If you choose to use FastPencil, the Publisher option is your best bet, especially if you plan to produce more than one book. Assemble an editorial team and have a professional cover designed to the FastPencil specifications. You'll be all set.

PressBooks.com offers another blog-to-book option. While you could blog on this site, I recommend importing your content by first exporting an XML file of the desired posts to your computer. (Export the blog posts in WordPress "Tools.") Then import the XML file into PressBooks. The site offers several design themes, and you can drag and drop your content easily to organize, format using your photos, and edit and revise in the program itself. Bringing in an editor is problematic unless she works directly in PressBooks. (That means she must know WordPress, since this system is built on this technology.) You also can add front matter and back matter. Once done, output a PDF for print use (or an .epub or .mobi file to produce an e-book). The service is free to try. When you're ready to publish, you pay $19 to remove the PressBooks watermark from the .epub and .mobi (for Kindle) files, or $99 to remove the watermark from the e-book and PDF files. They also offer full conversion service beginning at $350.

If you created a manuscript as you blogged your book, there are some other blog-to-book options to consider. www.TheBookDesigner.com's Book Design Templates for Microsoft Word are a super solution if want to save money on interior book design. You can quickly and efficiently create beautiful books right in Word. These templates are built to industry-standard specifications and are handcrafted by an award-winning book designer. (A number of designs also allow you to create e-books as well.)

I found Scrivener, a writing tool, an effective option for going from blog to book. It works if you have a Word manuscript prepared and ready to import to Scrivener or if you write and file your posts in Scrivener as you blog your book, basically creating your manuscript in Scrivener. After I discovered this tool, I began doing just that—writing and filing all my blog posts in Scrivener so I could compile them into books later. However, I also imported a huge manuscript (the full first edition of this book) and a smaller manuscript comprised of about four months of posts—in seconds. The system organized them for me by chapter, and I then was able to edit and revise in Scrivener, add new content, add research files, and "compile" (Scrivener's export function) as a Word document to give to my editor. You can import the edited version of your manuscript as a research document or copy and paste the new versions into new files and view them in a split screen to make the changes.

(Note: I write my blog posts using "multimarkdown," a way to write HTML without knowing coding, and use the "compile multimarkdown" → "webpage function" to produce formatted content for my blog posts. This saves me a ton of time.)

Additionally, Scrivener allows you to compile as a PDF. You then have a file to upload to CreateSpace or Ingram Spark. (Scrivener also compiles as .epub and .mobi files, making it a great tool for producing e-books as well. The files it produces tend to be devoid of bad code that causes e-book formatting problems.)

If you didn't produce a manuscript and are ready to turn your blogged book into a printed book, or you wrote all your blogged-book posts in WordPress and now want to book your blog, your first problem lies in getting content off your WordPress site and into Word. Book designers use Word docs to create printed books, editors use Word as well, and you need a Word doc to produce an e-book should you decide to do so. Despite hours of searching for a shortcut that avoids copying and pasting all your blog content into a Word doc, I have found just two solutions.

To turn blog posts into a Word file, try BlogBookMaker.com (also mentioned in chapter seven). It produces a document that includes your photos and that has been formatted to look like a book. The only drawback: The service costs $250 for just one week's use (for just one blog site). You can download as much content as you want in that time period. (Download it all!) Also, to use the service, verification of copyright ownership is required.

BlogBookMaker works with WordPress.org and WordPress.com as well as some Blogspot, Typepad, and custom blogging platforms (if you know the RSS Feed address). By selecting different categories (and *only* categories), which you set up in advance, you can create multiple books from your blog. This tool creates a linked table of contents automatically from heading tags in your posts, allows you to upload or link to book covers (and automatically centers and resizes them), allows for adding of front- and back matter, and has a drag-and-drop content re-ordering ability. Ultimately, you receive a Word 2010 .docx file that is automatically downloaded to your computer. This file can be edited further in Microsoft Word 2010 or higher, saved directly as a PDF file (and other formats), and uploaded to Kindle, CreateSpace, Ingram Spark, or many other publishing options. Although this service is costly, the additional draw is that it strips out all "junk code" that can cause formatting problems.

BlogBooker.com's beta service (also mentioned in chapter seven) is a second option. It also will produce a PDF or a .doc file of your blog content. I tried this service numerous times with the intent of consistently producing a Word file. Several times, however, I did not get

.doc output, just a PDF. Other times I received a file with an .odt file extension, which is given to office document text files created in the OpenOffice and StarOffice word processing applications. I was able to open these using a text editor and then copy and paste the content successfully into Word. On a few occasions, BlogBooker did provide a download of a nicely formatted .docx file, so I can say it works and is an option, but it seems to be hit or miss. That said, it's worth a try before you pay $250. I don't know if it leaves in any problematic code, however. This service is free and hopefully will get more reliable once out of the beta, or early, stage of development.

I did try converting the PDFs produced by BlogBooker.com with a variety of blog-to-book programs to Word, but these attempts were unsuccessful. This is an option, though, and there are plugins that produce a PDF from your WordPress content.

Once you have that printed book in hand, start selling it! Go back to what you've already learned about promotion.

TURNING YOUR BLOGGED BOOK INTO AN E-BOOK

If you don't want to incur much expense, you can simply convert your blogged book into an e-book and become an e-book publisher. In this way, you can enter the newest and fastest-growing area of the publishing industry. If you choose to take this route, you can sell your e-book from your blogged-book site, as well as from www.Amazon.com, www.BarnesandNoble.com, www.Apple.com, www.Kobo.com, www.Smashwords.com, and more, thus making it readily available for all e-readers.

It used to be that authors created e-books simply by making PDFs of Word documents. You can still do this and make your content available to your readers. Creating this type of e-book is simple, but you do need some design savvy. If you plan to charge a fair amount, you must create an e-book that looks nice and has decent graphics. After that, you need only get yourself a copy of Adobe Acrobat Professional or download a free PDF program like CutePDF. Save your finished manuscript as a secure PDF, and you are ready to sell it. (If you don't have any design ability, you can save your Word document, but it may not look pretty unless you opt to use a template.)

Many people ask if this PDF needs to be password protected, which means you must give the person who buys the e-book a password to open the document. This is supposed to curtail illicit sharing of the e-book. You can password protect it if you like; I've never yet purchased one that was. Most people treat e-books just like printed books, which are purchased and then lent out if they are well liked. Basically you want them to be shared or to go viral, if possible.

There are some terrifically easy ways to create e-books for all e-reader formats that cost almost nothing. For instance, you can upload your Word document to an e-book distributor and publisher, like Smashwords. If the formatting is correct, it will pass their conversion requirements and then become available in almost every e-reader format. (At the time of this printing, Smashwords had not yet set up an agreement with Amazon's Kindle; you have to upload to Kindle yourself.) You may, however, want to hire someone to make sure your Word document meets Smashword's requirements; this conversion can cost as little as $50, and a list of vendors who do this is available at the site. Additionally a style guide is available at Smashwords and on Kindle, and most people can follow it and create a document that passes Smashword's requirements. When I uploaded my first e-book, I followed the style guide and then asked someone on the list of vendors to check my work. I paid a minimal amount because I had done most of what was necessary (and learned a lot in the process). She tweaked a few things, and my document passed with flying colors.

Additionally you need a front cover design for your e-book. A print book designer can do this for you, or you can hire an e-book designer. E-book cover designers tend to be cheaper. I had a cover done for $50 for one of my e-books. Once the designer provides you with the high-resolution artwork, upload it to Smashwords. It appears as a thumbnail in the Smashwords catalog. (You need a designer who is aware of this fact.)

After your book has been loaded at Smashwords and approved, Smashwords begins distributing it for you and you begin selling books. For this service, they take a minimal percentage of the book's selling price.

You can find a similar distribution service at FastPencil; however, the conversion process has a fee attached. Other e-book publishers and distributors exist as well, like www.BookBaby.com. Check out their fees, royalty schedules, and distribution range.

If you choose to produce a POD book using Amazon's CreateSpace, for a small fee they will convert your book to a Kindle e-book as well. This is a great deal. Of course, you can just upload a file for an e-book to Amazon's Kindle program.

Combine the Smashwords service with the Amazon Kindle Direct Publishing (KDP) service to make sure your e-book is available to everyone. Upload your document and your artwork to KDP, too. The same person who did your conversion for Smashwords can prepare it for Kindle, which requires a .mobi file. Your cover designer can produce a cover that works for both sites. Then advertise on your blogged book's site that the e-book is available at all online bookstore locations.

If you prepared your e-book files (.mobi and .epub) using www.TheBookDesigner.com's Book Design Templates for Microsoft Word, note that the files may not work well for Smashwords.

If you use PressBooks to go from blog to e-book, you can take advantage of the site's partnership with www.BookBaby.com for book distribution. Utilize the "Sell" button that recommends BookBaby, a service that will get your book into eleven different e-book stores for a flat fee starting at $99 (with a 10 percent discount for PressBooks users and 100 percent royalties). Or you can upload to Kindle and Smashwords by yourself.

I tested out PressBooks to go from blog to book. Minus a few minor problems—a lost section header, some italics not maintained in the .mobi versions, and line-break hyphenations in some of my longer titles in the .epub file (before and after conversion)—the e-book files produced were usable. I know some self-publishing experts, such as Carla King, author of *Self-Publishing Boot Camp*, who swear by PressBooks for self-publishing e-books and print books, so I'd trust their experience over mine. (It could have been user error.)

While PressBooks allows you to produce e-book files (.mobi and .epub) that work well for Kindle, Nook, iBooks, etc., you can't print out a Word file, which makes it hard to create a file for Smashwords. I had trouble converting the PDF I exported to a Word file to use at Smashwords, which was another drawback of this tool (the inability to bring in an editor being the first).

Scrivener, on the other hand, produces .mobi files for Kindle, .epub files for all other e-book formats, and both Word and PDF files. That means you can format the Word file successfully after compiling (exporting) it using Smashword's style and upload to that site as well. (My e-book developer had some issues with the Smashwords [.epub] file again.) Gwen Hernandez, author of *Scrivener for Dummies*, created the .epub, .mobi, and PDF versions of her novel, *Blind Fury*, in Scrivener without any other program, and many other Scrivener users have similar stories. This requires some knowledge of the "compile" function, though, and getting the settings right can take some trial and error. Hernandez cautions that the Windows version doesn't yet support the alternating headers, footers, and margins (for creating different left/right pages) necessary to produce a PDF for CreateSpace. Therefore, Windows users (at this time) need to output to a Word doc, make the changes there, and then save as a PDF.

I've tried to output all four types of files somewhat successfully, and I know others who have done so with great success. Any complaints I've heard here and there from those creating e-books (or print books) with Scrivener, I believe, come from lack of compiling knowledge.

CAN YOU BLOG A BOOK AND USE THE AMAZON KDP AND KDP SELECT PROGRAMS?

When publishing on Amazon, you have two choices: Kindle Direct Publishing (KDP) and Kindle Direct Publishing Select (KDP Select). KDP is Amazon's basic publishing option. KDP Select offers some perks, such as the ability to promote your book with "free days" and to place your title in the lending library used by Amazon Prime members.

It's not uncommon for those blogging books and booking blogs to get scary notices from Amazon saying their title has been put on hold after they upload their books to the KDP program. One of my clients even had her whole account put on hold temporarily. I want you to be prepared and to understand what is happening. It does not mean that you can't publish your blogged book as an e-book using the Kindle platform.

When you finish your blogged book and decide to publish it as a Kindle e-book, you choose to use either the KDP or KDP Select program. The KDP Select program asks you to give Amazon exclusive rights to sell, or distribute, your book for ninety days. That means you do not have the right to sell it anywhere else in digital format during that time period. Notice that I used the word *rights*. You are giving away distribution rights when you opt for this program. What you gain is the ability to give your book away for free for a number of days during that exclusive period as a promotional tool or to provide readers with limited-time discounts through Kindle Countdown Deals. You also receive the promotional perk of having your book included in the Kindle Owners' Lending Library. However, your book will not have the opportunity to gain readership in the Apple iBookstore, Barnes & Noble, Kobo, or anywhere else until you leave the KDP Select program.

Additionally, if you choose the KDP Select program, you will have to remove from your site all but 10 percent of your blogged book, or only blog that percentage—which defeats the purpose of blogging it.

If it sounds as if I'm not a proponent of this program, you're right. You can read more about the reasons you might not want to use KDP Select from Smashwords founder Mark Coker in this post: blog.smash words.com/2012/11/amazon-grinch-who-stole-christmas.html).

Let's start with the basics: The claim you may have heard elsewhere that Amazon's KDP program does not allow publication of blogged material at all is false. As a blogger, you can choose to publish your blogged material in an e-book with the normal Kindle program (KDP) or the KDP Select program; both allow blogged material. (You also can use CreateSpace to produce a POD.) According to Brittany Turner, an Amazon representative, "KDP does allow writers to sell material previously published on the Internet, as long as they are the rights holder."

That said, know that you will be asked to prove that you own the rights to your blogged book.

When you upload your blogged book on Amazon as a KDP e-book, or even as a print book on CreateSpace, you will be asked when you fill out the application if you own the rights to the material. Later, once you've actually uploaded your document to the system, Amazon will discover the material in your book also exists on the Internet—on your blog. At that point, it will put a temporary hold on publication to determine if you do, indeed, hold the rights to the material. That's when you may receive a scary e-mail notifying you that this has occurred.

For example, one of my clients called me in a panic when her blogged book was not immediately approved as an Amazon Kindle book in the KDP program. She was on a deadline to get it released and was waiting for the approval to come through, but instead she received an e-mail telling her the book was under review. Subsequently, her Amazon account was blocked. A few days later her account was unblocked and the e-book was finally published, making her release late and causing her a fair amount of stress.

You can make sure your Amazon Kindle (or CreateSpace) experience is a pleasant one by understanding why things happen the way they do and being prepared for the process. Let's look at what normally happens and why.

Turner explains the process: "When submitting content that is also freely available on the Web (such as content from their blog), a temporary hold may be placed on the book until the author confirms they have publishing rights to the book and control where the book is distributed."

You then have to prove the content in your book came from your personal blog, and not someone else's blog, and that you do, indeed, have rights to the content and to decide how and where that content is distributed. "These should both be true for someone's personal blog," says Turner, which means you won't have a problem getting your blogged book approved via CreateSpace or through the KDP Program.

When you get that e-mail from Amazon saying your book has been placed on temporary hold and asking you to prove you are the rights holder, don't panic. Simply comply with Amazon's requests. (Remember, the fact that you blogged your book means getting one of these e-mails is inevitable if you self-publish using Amazon.) Here's what you will need to provide when that e-mail shows up.

1. the URLs for all websites where the content is published
2. an explanation as to why the content is available online

Turner noted that this information must be sent to Amazon within five days. "Once that occurs the book should be cleared for sale shortly after," she said. "If authors have questions they can always get in touch with us here: kdp.amazon.com/self-publishing/contact-us."

Don't expect to be able to call anyone with questions or to have a conversation. They won't call you either. Your only communication about the rights to your blogged material will be by e-mail.

I know finding your book on temporary hold may be disturbing—even annoying—but keep in mind that this action is to protect you. You wouldn't want someone to publish your blogged material in his or her book, right? To ensure that doesn't happen, Amazon verifies ownership of previously published material on the Internet.

It's all good ... and you can still publish your blogged book.

Now, KDP Select is a different story entirely if you have blogged your book or booked your blog.

When you sign up for the KDP Select program, you cannot distribute your e-book anywhere other than Amazon for at least three months—including on your blog. If you visit the site, you can read this explanation of the program's exclusive publishing agreement:

"When you choose KDP Select for a book, you're committing to make the digital format of that book available exclusively through KDP. During the period of exclusivity, you cannot distribute your book digitally anywhere else, including on your website, blogs, etc. However, you can continue to distribute your book in physical format, or in any format other than digital."

That means you can't upload it to other distributors, such as Smashwords, Barnes & Noble or BookBaby. The only retailer who can sell the e-book version of your booked blog or blogged book is Amazon—not even you. And the only people who will be able to read your e-book are those who own a Kindle or who use the free Kindle reading apps on their devices.

That explains why one of my blog readers left me a comment on the original post on this topic and explained that she contacted a Kindle Select rep and was told: "You may offer a sample, excerpt, or teaser of your KDP Select-enrolled book on your website, as long as it doesn't include a substantial portion of your book's content. Up to about 10 percent of the book's content is a reasonable amount.

"Keep in mind that a sample of your book is also available on your Amazon detail page, and we recommend linking to your detail page from your other sites.

"You may also put similar samples on other websites. We strongly recommend you clearly indicate in the title of your sample that it is a sample, so that there won't be confusion regarding availability of your book on another sales channel."

This book blogger received different information because she was asking about the KDP Select program, not the KDP program. As Turner pointed out when I asked her about these details, "The new case you're referring to is when that KDP book is then enrolled in KDP Select. KDP Select is an optional program where an author can choose to make their book exclusive to Kindle for ninety days. When an author chooses to enroll their book in KDP Select, they're committing to make the digital format of that book available exclusively through KDP. During the period of exclusivity, they cannot distribute their book digitally anywhere else, including on their website, blogs, etc. However, they can continue to distribute their book in physical format, or in any format other than digital."

What if you have blogged 75 or 85 percent of your book—the first draft minus a few chapters—just as I've taught you to do? If you enroll in the KDP Select program, rather than the KDP program, that's a real problem.

I realize, as you probably do, too, that having the blogged version of your book published on your blog doesn't technically represent "selling" your book. You may not even think of it as distributing the book. The people at Amazon don't see the distinction. They also don't care that the version on your blog is the first draft, is different from the final e-book version because it hasn't been revised and edited, and has 25 percent less content. Their rules are hard and fast: You must have only 10 percent of the book online at the same time that you have your e-book for sale in the KDP Select program.

Think about that … what will you do with the other 65 or 75 percent during that time? Take it down and create a ton of 404 (Not Found) errors, which are created when the server can't find what was requested? I don't think so. Shut down your blog? Then why did you bother blogging it in the first place? And, as I said, blogging just 10 percent won't build you a platform. (It would test-market your idea to some extent, but that's about it.)

I'll reiterate: If you publish your finished blogged book as an Amazon Kindle e-book (KDP), not as a KDP Select e-book, you can distribute your book using other channels, and you can keep all those precious posts intact and published on your blog. You won't have lost any rights, and you can continue enjoying the fruits of your blogging labor as well as the benefits of having a Kindle e-book.

Okay! You're now ready to produce a book from your blog—no matter whether you blogged or booked it or decided to take the traditional or indie route.

If all these options for turning your blogged book into something more tangible haven't set your mind reeling, here's something else to think about: Creating a printed or e-book really just comes down to recycling, or repurposing, your writing into another form—one that brings in income. Books, however, represent only one way to do that. Are you ready to explore other means of putting all that content you created to use? Then move on to the next chapter.

CHAPTER 10

HOW TO REPURPOSE YOUR BLOG POSTS FOR PROFIT AND PROMOTION

Here's a bit of information the book industry doesn't like to reveal: Books don't provide a huge source of income. In fact, most authors, with the exception of those who consistently hit the bestseller lists, supplement their book royalties with additional sources of income that may or may not be related to their publishing efforts. As an author and a blogger who has just produced or may be in the process of producing amazing amounts of content, you have a great advantage: You can turn all that content into money-making products. These "information products" can provide you with multiple streams of income and a business that revolves around your book. You can become an *authorpreneur* or a *blogpreneur*. Many nonfiction books lend themselves to this.

You might have picked up this book so you could begin blogging your book from start to finish and get discovered by an agent or a publisher along the way. Or you may have stumbled upon it after you already began blogging. Maybe you've been blogging for a while and achieved some success, which led you to wonder, *Could I turn my blog into a book?*

Possibly you thought about some of those blog-to-book success stories, like *Julie & Julia* or *Stuff White People Like*, and thought, *That could be me. I could get discovered, too.*

It could be that you began blogging a book on a new blog after you created a successful blog on another topic. Now you have more than one source of valuable content. Or you haven't blogged a book, but you have an existing blog with a lot—a whole lot—of blog content you could put to use and that may not fit into just one book. Now you need to figure out how to recycle, or repurpose, all that content for profit as well as for promotion.

Each time you create an information product, you can sell it and advertise it on your blog and through all your social networks. Plus, you can create products, like a special report, and give them away as enticements for readers to join your mailing list or subscribe to your blog. Thus, your information products become promotional tools as well as income producers.

CREATE RELATED INFORMATION PRODUCTS FOR MULTIPLE STREAMS OF INCOME

Information products provide consumers with the information they need or want, solve problems, offer expert advice, educate, or in some way provide a service, tip, or tool. The information is packaged in a variety of ways and sold, usually on the Internet, via a website. This makes your blog, which is a website, the perfect place from which to promote and sell these products.

Your blog provides a treasure trove of gems to turn into information products. You can turn the jewels—in this case, posts—into special reports, videos, recordings (MP3s, CDs, or DVDs), e-books, workbooks, teleseminars, webinars, home-study courses, or online courses. You also can create related services, such as coaching and consulting. If you've finished blogging your book, are currently blogging it, or even have simply been blogging with no thought until now of a book, information products can provide you with great income sources. Often they provide passive income—the products sell "while you sleep," and you wake up to money in the bank.

Your blogged, printed, or digital book shouldn't be your only source of income; if it is, you might find yourself earning less than you'd like. Instead, think like a businessperson or entrepreneur. Become an authorpreneur or blogpreneur. Use your book to create multiple streams of income.

Here's how you start: First, you need a mechanism for selling your information products. You can create a page on your website (blog) with a shopping cart system so readers or visitors can purchase these items any time, day or night, by downloading them. You may want to sign up for a service like 1ShoppingCart.com so an auto-responder sends the purchased items immediately, or simply use www.PayPal.com and send them out manually. There are ways to hook up PayPal with mailing list services, like www.AWeber.com, and use their auto-responders to send out products, but it's more complicated. You also can use E-junkie.com or www.ClickBank.com. These services deliver digital downloads. Like PayPal, they provide a code you place on your site that creates "buy buttons," and the rest is handled via their services.

Second, look at your manuscript or blog and look for topics or content to expand.

- What blogged-book posts, or posts in general, might be subjects of their own?
- What topics could be made into a series of posts?
- What topics have you blogged about that generated a lot of interest from your readers in the form of comments or queries (or traffic)?
- What topic did you want to cover that didn't fit into the scope of your blogged book or of a particular chapter and that you could craft into an article, blog post, or some other type of content?
- What questions do you frequently get asked?

The answers to these questions all might generate ideas for good information products.

Third, look at your manuscript for topics you already have covered as a series of posts. Maybe you wrote five posts on a particular subject that lends itself to a special report or to a course of some sort. Do your readers want to learn how to do whatever you were writing about? If so, this could work as a product.

TYPES OF INFORMATION PRODUCTS

What types of information products might you create? Here's a quick list.

1. Tip Sheets, Books, or Booklets

Do you offer a lot of tips on your blog? Do you have a lot of great advice in the posts of your blogged book? Pull these into a tip sheet that consists solely of beneficial advice in little snippets. Include twenty tips on a page, and convert it into a PDF. Or compile thirty days' worth of tips or one hundred tips and turn this into a short book or booklet. If you have a bit more to say, consider producing a tip booklet that offers one tip per page with a little bit of copy explaining the tip. You can publish them inexpensively as a PDF, an e-book, or a printed and saddle-stitched (stapled) booklet.

You may be able to produce other kinds of booklets based on your blog content as well. If you can find a printer with a booklet press, these products cost just dollars to produce. You send off a PDF, and voilà! You have a booklet. Like POD, you can print one or one thousand. A short book (sixty pages or less) can be produced inexpensively on a booklet press in most cases. Depending on page count, in some cases you also might produce these as POD books or as printed books produced on short-run digital presses.

2. Special Reports

You can produce a special report on almost anything. These are short, informative documents, usually under ten pages, on one highly focused topic. Often they are written for professionals. For example, I created one on how to build author platform; I sell it for $10, and I used to give it away to those who signed up for my mailing list. I created it out of a number of blog posts I edited together, along with a little extra copy to flesh it out. Create a cover, and you're in business. (Explore services like www.Canva.com or www.Fiverr.com for free or inexpensive ($5) ways to create or commission cover art.)

Mine your blogged book or your blog for content that lends itself to a special report. What do your readers want or need to know? What problem can you solve for them? What could you tell them in a few short pages? Maybe something interesting, new, or newsworthy has happened that relates to your blogged book; this could be additional content used for a special report, and then you could promote your blogged book (or blog) by publicizing the report for sale at your blogged-book site (and promote your book at the end of the special report).

3. Videos and Recordings

I mentioned videos and how to create them for YouTube in chapter eight. You also can create educational videos and sell them, and the same goes for audio recordings. Plus, I highly recommend you videotape or record almost everything you do—teleseminars, webinars, workshops, Google Hangouts on Air, speeches, and radio interviews. You then can sell them or use them in some other way as information products.

Creating audio recordings is simple: Purchase a decent digital recorder, and record yourself reading blog posts, talking about your blogged book, or telling people how to do different things related to the topic of your blogged book. Or record on your computer or smart phone (but purchase a good mic). Sell these recordings as products—MP3s and such. Or put them on CDs and package them as a product. (You also can upload them on blog posts so people can listen to them, and you can then let them know that more such audio recordings are available for sale.) Consider starting a podcast; these have become quite popular, and they consist primarily of audio recordings uploaded to iTunes and other such sites (but also available as audio and/or video on your blog). There are easy audio-editing programs available online, such as Audacity, and Adobe offers Audition. Macs come with Garageband. If you are working with video, you can start with Moviemaker and iMovie or try Camtasia or Adobe Premier Pro.

4. Home-Study and Online Courses

If your book lends itself to teaching, demonstrations, or classes, consider combining some of your blog posts or special reports with your audio and video to create home-study or online courses. Or create a workbook from some of your blogged-book or blog material and combine it with audio and video. You can do this without the audio and video as well; just use a printed workbook or some sort of online program you facilitate via e-mail auto-responders. You also can combine a workbook with teleseminars, workshops, or coaching. People pay a lot of money for online courses and home-study programs.

5. Coaching and Consulting

If your blogged book or blog offers great information that teaches people about how to do something, or if it focuses on some sort of system for accomplishing a task or goal, consider providing coaching and consulting services. Advertise them on your blog or website. (By the way, if you want to do this, get that printed book out right away. Nothing will give you more credibility as an expert than becoming the author of a printed book.)

6. Books

We've already spoken a great deal about books. Here I'd like to discuss one facet of turning blogs into books: how to turn your blog into a book production machine. After all, books are products.

Once you know how to blog a book, you can blog long books *and* short books. The short books are your ticket to branding, expert status, platform, customers and clients, and cash! Today, you can produce 4,000- to 20,000- word e-books on Kindle, so do not think magnum opus!

Just as you planned out the posts for a longer book, brainstorm a short book—a series of ten to thirty posts. Once you've published these on your blog, repurpose them into an e-book or a print-on-demand book.

I did this with my book *10 Days and 10 Ways to Return to Your Best Self: A T'shuvah Tool Bridging Religious Traditions*. I took ten blog posts I'd written as a series, added an introduction and conclusion, edited the copy, and then tacked on some promotional material for my other short books at the end. When done, I had a seventy-two-page book I printed on a short-run digital press and then at CreateSpace as well.

I recently took twelve posts I wrote as a series, added additional posts on the same topic, created a bit of new content for an intro and conclusion, and published an e-book called *The Nonfiction Book Proposal De-mystified: An Easy-Schmeasy Guide to Writing a Business Plan for Your Book*. I then released *Authorpreneur: How to Build a Business Around Your Book*. (This is a great resource, by the way, for producing any of the products or services mentioned in this chapter.) It was followed by *Blog-preneur: How to Build a Business Around Your Blog* and *Blogging Basics for Aspiring Authors*, both of which were blogged consciously as series to be turned into books later.

Think about how easy it becomes to produce books from blogged content if you plan those posts as a series you know you will turn into a book—and how much better those books will be in the end than if you booked them. Plus, you can plan out a few related series of posts, publish them as e-books, and then combine them later into a full-length book.

7. Giveaways

Any of these books or smaller products can become giveaways to help you build your mailing list. You even can excerpt material from your blogged book as a free enticement to sign up. Package it as something new and interesting. Add a video or audio element to it and offer it as a free gift to mailing list subscribers.

8. Membership Sites and Continuity Programs

If you've ever purchased a course and had to have login credentials to access it, that information product likely was hosted on a membership site. If you've joined a membership site, such as my Nonfiction Writers' University or Michael Hyatt's Platform University, all the information, including the forum, is provided via a membership site. In fact, you can provide your customers with your products and services via member-ship sites, and they won't even know they've "joined."

If you decide to create a variety of courses or to produce a conti-nuity program such as a "university," an association, or an organiza-tion that requires yearly or monthly payment to become a member, you need a membership site plugin. A variety of them exist, such as Wishlist, MemberPress, Restrict Content Pro, MemberMouse, and Mag-ic Member, to name just a few. These plugins provide you with password-protected pages and landing pages that allow you to place all your content—videos, audio recordings, workbooks, reports, forums, etc.—in a secure place that only those who pay can access.

BROADCAST YOUR BOOK

I would be remiss not to mention the fact that, as a blogger, you should consider "broadcasting" your book with a podcast or Google Hangouts on Air. These give you two more ways to drive traffic to your blog and develop more fans and subscribers, platform, visibility, and expert status, all of which will help you achieve your goals as you write your book. That's right ... apply the same exact strategy used to blog a book to podcasting or producing live recorded video events.

Podcasting a book works exactly like blogging.

1. Go through all the steps outlined in this book.
2. Once you have chunked down your book into post-sized bits, use those posts as the basis for your podcast scripts.
3. After you record a show, transcribe it into a word processing document.
4. Compile all transcripts into one document—your manuscript-in-the-making.
5. Edit each podcast transcript.
6. Use the transcript as show notes (a blog post that also hosts the audio) and as part of your manuscript.

I've heard stories of people podcasting books. Most have actually written their books first and then broadcast them or repurposed the content from their podcasts (booked a podcast). They haven't consciously podcast a whole book start to finish from scratch. Best-selling author, entrepreneur, and marketing expert Mike Koenigs uses his successful podcast as the content source for almost all of his books. Mignon Fogarty of the *Grammar Girl* blog did a combination of booking her blog and booking her podcast when she created her best-selling books. Author J.C. Hutchins podcast his novels and landed a publishing deal with St. Martin's Press. Scott Sigler podcasted his way to a five-book deal with

Crown Publishing. This can be a way to monetize your book and to promote it prior to release—and to get noticed by an agent or a publisher.

You can do the same thing with webinars or Google Hangouts on Air. Follow the six steps outlined on the previous page and write your book as broadcast sessions. With webinars, you can host them alone, which creates a manuscript filled with your content alone. If you choose a Hangout (which, by the way, gets great Google exposure) you can interview other experts; this is a common format for Hangouts on Air. This associates your name with these thought leaders, gets them on board to help pre-promote your book, and helps you research your topic. Your transcripts, however, will be a mix of their information and yours. If you want to produce a book that features interviews, this will work great! If not, you'll have a harder time editing your transcripts into a book, so think about the format of your show before you begin.

By always considering how to work smarter, not harder—looking for ways to repurpose material as you create it—you can produce not just one book but many over time. After all, blogging, podcasting, Hangouts on Air, product creation, and promotion are long-term activities that often take writers away from writing … but that doesn't have to be the case. They can become the source of more books if you are creative.

No matter what type of products and services you choose to produce, be sure you promote them well. Most membership plugins offer templates or ways to create sales pages, or splash pages. You might want to invest in something like LeadPages.com, however, which offers professional templates.

Then there's the need to launch each product. Just as you launch a book, you launch your products and services for the best results. To learn more about this, read Jeff Walker's *Launch* and generally educate yourself on how to succeed as an online marketer. Authorpreneurs and blogpreneurs throw themselves into the pit with everyone else selling online. To do that well, you have to learn best marketing practices.

All the products mentioned here—and others you may think of that I have not mentioned—work for you night and day, 24/7, if you set up a great storefront in cyberspace. That's the beauty of a blog and information products working together. It's a way to leverage your knowledge. And here's the fabulous thing: The more people come to use and to love all your products and services, the more people will buy your book.

CHAPTER 11

BLOG-TO-BOOK SUCCESS STORIES

If you want to learn how to succeed at anything in life, ask those who have already achieved success how they did so. Create a road map from their success stories. Ask them for tips and advice. Allow them to mentor you, even if they only answer your questions. Then emulate them as best you can in your own unique way.

Increasingly more people write books from start to finish using blog technology. In November 2014, during National Nonfiction Writing Month (NaNoWriMo), 7 percent of the registered participants chose to blog books, which tells me this method of writing books continues to gain popularity. (You can find many in-process blogged books here: HowToBlogABook.com/List-Your-Book.) Since the release of the first edition of this book, however, I have found few blogged-book traditional publishing success stories to highlight. That doesn't mean none exist!

Despite the fact that at this time it remains easier to report on bloggers who have landed book deals—the blog-to-book success stories we all have heard so much about—in this chapter you'll hear directly from both people who have blogged their books and those who have booked their blogs successfully. You'll learn from four bloggers who blogged their books and chose to self-publish. They all achieved success based on their own definition and the fact that they reached their goals. You'll also find interviews with five bloggers who landed blog-to-book deals and booked their blogs. All five have had tremendous success with their blogs and, subsequently, with their books as well.

Read on and learn.

JEANNIE DAVIDE-RIVERA ON BLOGGING HER BOOK: *TWIRLING NAKED IN THE STREETS AND NO ONE NOTICED*

Author, student, and stay-at-home mother Jeannie Davide-Rivera stumbled through life with a form of autism called Asperger's Syndrome (AS). She raised four sons, three of whom are on the autism spectrum. Her blog, AspieWriter.com, is dedicated to her experiences living with and raising children on the autism spectrum. "I began my blog in the beginning of my discovery process, when I was learning what had been 'wrong' with me my entire life," she explains. "Talking with other adult woman on the spectrum, I realized that although there were many others 'like' me, there was not that much written material about or especially by autistic women. That is when I determined that I would write my story in the hopes that someone else would read it and say, 'No way. Me too!'"

Her book, *Twirling Naked in the Streets and No One Noticed: Growing up with Undiagnosed Autism*, is a memoir that both describes Davide-Rivera's life growing up and teaches others about autism spectrum disorders. Shortly after publication, the book won the 2013 International Reader's Favorites Award in the autobiography category.

Why did you decide to blog a book?

I came across a post on Cathy C. Hall's blog (c-c-hall. com/2014/06/11/read-and-learn-grasshopper-nina-amir-and-the-author-training-manual) in which you [Nina Amir] were the guest blogger. In the post, you described your own book, *How to Blog a Book*, and it immediately sounded like something I wanted to pursue. I made many visits to your website after that day and began writing my book—well, blogging the book—during November [National Nonfiction Writing Month]. The most important part of blogging the book for me was my readers' responses and the fact that they awaited the next installments. These two factors kept me focused and returning to my keyboard day after day.

What process did you use to plan out your blogged book?

My process was fairly simple, since a memoir is much like writing fiction—only the story is true. I outlined what I wanted to write by sorting the story into scenes. I wrote each scene and subject I wanted to cover about autism on index cards, and then I got to work.

How often did you publish posts, and how long did it take you to blog your first draft?

I published posts almost every day or at the least every other day. It took me from November until February to complete my first draft, which was accomplished in approximately one hundred blog posts.

How much new content did you later add to your book? Did you plan for this content in advance (leave it out purposely on the blog), or was it simply added during the editing process?

I did not really add any new content to the book later—only what was required during the editing process. This included creating transitions from scene to scene and combining posts into chapters so the work would read like a book and not a series of blog posts. That said, I wrote in a very straightforward manner, chronologically, so there was not too much manuscript manipulation needed.

How much editing was necessary to complete your blogged book and make it flow?

There was not very much editing necessary because the story I wrote was already planned out and set in a format appropriate to a memoir. Most revisions were grammatical in nature.

Did you run into any writing or editing problems particular to blogging a book?

I did not; in fact, I found blogging my story to be freeing, if not terrifying. It forced me to write it and let it go out into the world without fretting *too* much. I tend to fall into some serious analysis paralysis, and blogging eliminated much of that as well.

Did blogging a book make you a better writer?

Definitely! It forced me to write my thoughts in a concise manner. Being ever aware of the word count constraints of writing blog posts (readers tend not to read extensive posts), I was forced to choose my words wisely and home in on the most important things I needed to say. That said, my posts did not adhere to the standard 400 to 600 words but ran an average of 1,000 to 1,200 words.

Did blogging your book make you a better blogger? Did it improve your blog in any way?

I actually began a separate blog specifically to write my book, which was connected to my *Aspie Writer* blog but was not a part of it. When I proceeded to publish my book on Amazon using the KDP Select program, I was required to take the blog down to pass their publishing process (only 10 percent of your work can be available on your website). This made me extremely glad that I kept a separate blog; it was easier to take it offline. I then posted excerpts from my book (previous blog posts) on my main blog, which a different audience was reading and that facilitated book promotion.

Do you have three to five tips you can offer about how to blog a book?

Have a plan; write an outline, even a short one, to give you a direction. Post regularly; although I posted every day to every other day, readers still wanted more—quickly. When possible, write many posts in one sitting, and then schedule them to post throughout the week. This will free you up a little so you can breathe when you need to. But beware—what propelled me forward was knowing that the readers were waiting.

What one thing did you do that increased your traffic or brought in more unique visitors?

> I began to write for other websites, as well as to guest blog. That allowed me to reach new readers on a fairly consistent basis. Additionally, offering other bloggers my book for free in return for an honest review helped bring many additional visitors as well.

How long did it take for you to gain blog readers, and can you pinpoint any certain event that created a tipping point when readership increased noticeably?

> I cannot pinpoint any tipping point but can say that readership increased steadily through the course of writing my book, and many have followed to my "main" blog and remain readers and/or followers today.
>
> Also, my social network contacts (Facebook and Twitter) increased as my blog readers increased. I would even say they increased much faster than the blog readers did. Additionally, as I posted more articles related to autism, other websites began to pick up pieces of my writing (*BBC News, Psychology Today, Thinking Person's Guide to Autism*) which increased traffic and unique visitors significantly.

Why did you decide to go the indie route?

> I lack the patience to attempt to sell a manuscript to a traditional publisher. In addition, most of the work—writing, designing, promoting—would still fall on me as the author, and, therefore, it did not make much sense to pursue traditional publishing. I am very happy with my decision, as I am certain that I make more money in royalties from my work than I would have from going traditional.

What's the most important thing a blogger can do to get noticed in the blogosphere and to build an author platform or fan base?

> Connect with other like-minded bloggers! This is the number one contributing factor I can pinpoint when it comes to getting noticed and getting your work out there. I con-

nected with many wonderful bloggers who were willing to
share my posts across their social media networks.

BRIAN CORMACK CARR ON BLOGGING HIS BOOK: *HOW TO FIND YOUR VITAL VOCATION*

Brian Cormack Carr's blog *Vital Vocation* (VitalVocation.com), originally was an online modular coaching program that could be accessed
by his coaching clients and the readers of his main blog, *Your Wise Life*
(www.CormackCarr.com). After participants in the program and readers of his primary blog prompted him to do more writing, he decided to repurpose the coaching program into his first book and started
blogging *How to Find Your Vital Vocation: A Practical Guide to Dis-
covering Your Career Purpose and Getting a Job You Love.*

Carr, a certified career coach and chief executive of Birmingham
Voluntary Service Council's (BVSC) The Centre for Voluntary Action
(one of the UK's leading local charities), says his book is "designed to
help anyone—whether a job hunter, career changer, or small-business
builder—to find the work of their dreams. It guides readers to get back
in touch with their gifts and talents and to help them use those to build
a lifestyle in which they are able to make a living and pursue their passions. As well as giving guidance on how to discover those passions,
it provides a range of tools and techniques to help readers put those
passions into practice." His blog, which contained 60 percent of the
book at the time—and more now—does the same.

Why did you decide to blog a book?

I had already been blogging for about three years as a way
of promoting my then-new coaching practice. I also had
written an online modular career coaching program. The
process of doing these things had reminded me that writing was really my first love and that I had a long-held am-
bition to write a book. So with encouragement from blog
readers and coaching clients who wanted to read more of
my writing, I decided to write the career guide that had

been forming in my mind and heart for several years. I set myself a goal of publishing the book before I turned forty. (And I did it with four days to spare!)

I did it partly by repurposing the material in the career-coaching program and the parts of my blog that related to careers and life purpose. I also converted what had been the coaching program website into a new blog so that I could focus on promoting the career-coaching element of my work and, thus, build up an audience for the book when it eventually came out. Inevitably, some material began to find its way both onto the blog and into the book, and it was around this time that I came across *How to Blog a Book,* which made me realize that I could actually do the whole thing in a much more systematic way.

What process did you use to plan out your blogged book?

It was a mixture of my own somewhat ramshackle process and the one that you outline so clearly in your book. I had already been moving previous blog posts into the book, along with the redrafted coaching-program modules, which were generally repurposed into chapters in the book. I also began posting excerpts of the book's manuscript onto the blog. Admittedly, this was really due to time constraints in the first instance. I have a very busy full-time job as CEO of a local charity, so my coaching work and writing were really very enjoyable sidelines, and I had to be careful to manage my time well. Writing all-new blog material *and* a book of separate material would have been too much, so it made sense to have the overlap. However, *How to Blog a Book* helped me do all this much more purposefully. I planned out the shape of the book and what material I'd need to write about, and I made myself a timetable of when I'd publish the same material (in smaller chunks) on the blog.

How often did you publish posts, and how long did it take you to blog your first draft?

I have to confess, I didn't publish posts nearly as often as I would have liked—mainly due to the time constraints mentioned above. Some weeks I managed one post, some weeks a couple, and some weeks none. What was most striking, however, was that even doing what I did, which was necessarily limited, allowed me to make great progress in building my social media presence *and* building an audience for the book. It's exciting to think about what would be possible if I'd had more time to be consistent in my application of the *How to Blog a Book* process.

How much new content did you later add to your book? Did you plan for this content in advance (leave it out purposely on the blog), or was it simply added during the editing process?

The book consists of around 56 percent all-new material. This is partly due to the fact that I didn't put all the sections on the blog I had intended to; I published several of them on the blog after the book's publication, however. But it also was partly deliberate. I did make a conscious decision that my book would be at least 50 percent new material. I wanted those readers who were following the blog to have a specific incentive to buy the book.

How much editing was necessary to complete your blogged book and make it flow?

Most of the editing involved creating transitions and connecting paragraphs. Much of the actual blog content worked well within the book, partly because I was conscious while blogging that I was "blogging a book," so I wrote with the eventual book's readership in mind.

Did you run into any writing or editing problems particular to blogging a book?

The main sticking points came in making decisions about how to split the material into blog-sized chunks. If anything, I think my blog posts were over-long because I tended to think more "book" than "blog" and didn't have as much time as I'd have liked to make the writing fit more into a blog context. However, I'm not too unhappy about this, because several people have told me that they bought my book *because* they liked the writing style on the blog. (One reader said, "I like that you write like a writer, not a blogger!") I think this is an example of where you have to—to some extent anyway—let your own style find its way out.

Did you incorporate your readers' comments before the manuscript went to press, and did they affect the final version of the book? Did you crowdsource feedback in any other way?

I did—mainly in terms of which topics got the biggest response in the blog. Those were the topics I tended to give more space to in the book. I also revised some sections significantly for the book based on reader feedback on the blog. Undoubtedly, this is one of the very best reasons to blog a book. How many other writers can get such immediate reader feedback? It's a fantastic way of making sure you really are connecting with your readership.

In terms of crowdsourcing, I didn't specifically do this during the writing process, but I did run a "crowdsourcing competition" on my blog to choose the cover of the book. That was fun, and it generated a lot of interest both in the book and the blog.

Did blogging a book make you a better writer?

I think so, mainly because it made me more attentive to my readership. Also, it disciplined me to organize myself in terms of timescales and the space I'd give to various topics in the book.

Did blogging your book make you a better blogger? Did it improve your blog in any way?

I don't consider myself a great blogger; I'm just not able to give it enough time. That said, blogging a book really did help me with the blog because it gave me a steady stream of relevant, content-rich material. My blog readership increased, as did positive feedback on my blog posts (after I started blogging the book).

What advice would you offer to aspiring writers who might want to blog a book?

Do it! It really is worthwhile, because either way you're going to be able to raise your profile and the profile of your book. I blogged some of the book before publication, which grew an audience for the book before it was published and enabled it to enter the Kindle bestsellers chart upon release, and I've been blogging parts of it after publication, which has kept my blog alive and continues to effectively promote the book.

Do you have three to five tips you can offer from your experience on how to blog a book?

1. Get organized. I kind of ploughed in first and started getting organized later. Next time, I'll be better prepared.
2. Start blogging early. Building an "author platform" is a great idea for any writer, particularly one (like me) who chooses to self-publish. The sooner you can start drawing people to your blog, the sooner you're going to be able to launch your book to a good reception.
3. Keep blogging after the book is published. If you're blogging your book as you write it, you might be tempted to see the book publication date as the end target. However, it's possible—even likely—that you'll have some new material in the book. Why not put that on the blog after the book's publication as a further way of promoting it?

What one thing did you do that increased your traffic or brought in more unique visitors?

During the process of blogging the book, and immediately after the book's publication, I made a real effort to gain some guest-posting opportunities and interviews on other blogs. I think getting traffic from other like-minded and supportive bloggers is always going to help draw more traffic to your blog (and your book). The great thing about blogging a book is that you can talk about that process. It's not how most people write a book, so it's an interesting topic.

How long did it take for you to gain blog readers, and can you pinpoint any certain event that created a tipping point when readership increased noticeably?

I already had a small readership from my previous blog and from my e-newsletter, so I wasn't starting from scratch. However, the process of blogging the book definitely boosted my online presence. My followers more than doubled during that period, and I saw the biggest jumps as soon as I started systematically publishing extracts from the book as I was writing it. Another jump came when I crowdsourced the cover of my book and then again when the book was published.

Can you offer any statistics on how your unique visitors or page views increased as you published posts related to your book? Did your social network contacts increase as well?

Yes, there was a very clear benefit here. My readership—composed of blog readers, e-newsletter subscribers, and social media followers—more than doubled. At the point when the book came out, I had grown a fairly small following to around eight hundred Twitter followers, six hundred Facebook fans, and a mailing list of about two hundred subscribers. Since the book's publication, Twitter followers and Facebook fans have almost doubled.

Did you use your blog analytics in any special manner when it came to refining your content?

This has been a weak spot for me! I did look at the analytics, but mainly out of interest rather than as information that prompted changes to what I was doing. That's partly down to my inexperience, and partly down to time constraints. I'm definitely going to pay more attention to this next time round.

Why did you decide to go the indie route?

I wanted to have the freedom to go at my own pace. Also, this started as a hobby for me (I already have a full-time job with which I'm very happy), so I was content to do it at my own pace. I'm working on my second book now, which I intend both to blog and to self-publish. After that, I intend to investigate the option of a traditional publishing deal.

What's the most important thing a blogger can do to get noticed in the blogosphere and to build an author platform or fan base?

Without a doubt, connect with other bloggers. Commenting on other blogs, offering to guest post on other blogs (or to host guest bloggers on your own), and seeking opportunities for interviews with other bloggers are all good ideas. The main thing is to be helpful, friendly, and sociable.

Has publishing a book affected your blog, business, or published book in any way?

It really has. My following as an author has grown exponentially, and inquiries for my coaching practice experienced a very healthy jump. [One of his initial intentions when he decided to blog a book was to promote his coaching services.] The biggest benefit, though, is that the whole process has taken me from being a part-time blogger to a published author. How amazing is that? It was a lot of fun on the way, and I learned a great deal. I can't wait to get started on my second blogged book!

GREGORY MARCUS ON BLOGGING HIS BOOK: *BUSTING CORPORATE IDOLS*

Gregory Marcus not only blogged a book; he built a business around that book. Recovering workaholic and life coach as well as stay-at-home dad, "Dr. Greg" Marcus says too many people have turned their employers into false idols. The blogged version of *Busting Your Corporate Idol: Self-Help for the Chronically Overworked*, which explains his metaphor of corporate idolatry and how people, circumstances, and corporate culture contribute to chronic overwork, is longer than the e-book and print editions. Marcus removed many posts from the final manuscript based on reader feedback and blog traffic. On the flip side, he said he included Tips and Tricks at the end of every chapter "to make it easier for people to digest and implement the lessons taught in the chapter." The blog and the book, which he self-published, helped him later land a literary agent for his second book.

Why did you decide to blog a book?

I had been working on the book for three years and was stuck with a few sample chapters and a detailed outline that I had revised a few times. I decided to blog the book to get a regular process and discipline to complete the book.

What process did you use to plan out your blogged book?

Since I had the outline and chapter one already written, I could get started almost right away. I also had an existing blog that I had started only a few months earlier.

How often did you publish posts, and how long did it take you to blog your first draft?

I committed to writing three to four posts a week, which I held to for six months. I think I dropped to two posts a week for the final two months, so overall I finished in eight months.

How much new content did you later add to your book? Did you plan for this content in advance (leave it out purposely on the blog), or was it simply added during the editing process?

I did not purposely leave anything out of the blogging process. I added a set of tips and Q&A at the end of each chapter.

How much editing was necessary to complete your blogged book and make it flow? What kind of revisions were necessary to make the blog posts work in the final draft?

I needed editing on a few levels—one to "de-blog" the book, which involved creating flow and transitions. It went pretty quickly and mostly involved removing phrases like "in the last post." Then I did a pretty detailed editing process to add and subtract content to tell the best story.

Did you incorporate your readers' comments before the manuscript went to press? How did comments affect the final version of the book?

I looked in detail at the number of page views each post had. I had fewer readers for chapters two and three of the book, which led to a complete rewrite of chapter two and a heavy edit of chapter three. I was also biased towards posts that had a lot of readers.

Did blogging a book make you a better writer?

Yes, because it gave me the discipline to write almost every day and to keep moving forward. Previously, I got too caught up in editing as I wrote, which slowed me down.

Did blogging your book make you a better blogger? Did it improve your blog in any way?

The traffic on my blog was way up while I was blogging the book. I had over fifteen thousand unique visitors during the nine months I blogged the book, up from a few thousand in the six prior months. I rarely post to the blog today, so understandably traffic is way, way down.

What advice would you offer to aspiring writers who might want to blog a book?

Have a clear goal in mind. For me, I knew the book that I wanted to write. The goal of blogging was to gain the discipline to write every day with the bonus of building awareness and a platform.

Do you have three to five tips you can offer from your experience on how to blog a book?

1. Pay attention to where your traffic comes from. I got a

lot of traffic from LinkedIn, which makes sense because
I was writing about overwork in the corporate world.
Focus your outreach to the networks that work.

2. Start working on finding an editor, etc., before you finish.
It takes time to vet editors, and I lost a few months after I
was done with the book trying to decide who should do
my editing.

3. As you are finishing, plan on continuing to post on your
blog. It doesn't have to be as often, but try to do it once a
week to keep in touch with your platform. I went to once
a month, and by the time I had a book to sell, my readers
had moved on to other things.

4. Pay attention to the title of your posts. Good titles make
a huge difference in traffic and also make good section
headers in the final book.

What one thing did you do that increased your traffic or brought in more unique visitors?

I had a lot of success posting in LinkedIn groups. I also
sent a message to every one of my LinkedIn contacts with
the title of my first post and a link. It was a great title, and
it drew in a lot of people immediately.

Can you offer any statistics on how your social network contacts increased?

	Pre-Book	End of Book
LinkedIn	520	1,032
Twitter	90	485

Why did you decide to go the indie route?

I had already been through one round of rejections from
agents and publishers. I wanted to get the book out as
quickly as possible, and I didn't think a traditional publisher had that much to offer me.

After the release of Busting Your Corporate Idol, you acquired a literary agent for a new book idea. Did blogging a book

help you accomplish this goal, and why did you decide to try traditional publishing again?

Blogging a book helped me because I would not have finished my first book if I hadn't blogged it. Having a published book was a huge credibility boost for me. There were a few reasons why I decided to try traditional publishing again. First, I'm not in as big a hurry for the second book, because I still have the business from the first book. In addition, my new book is targeting a Jewish readership, and I think I could benefit from the traditional publishing distribution for this market. In addition, it was a lot of work to find the editor, designer, cover designer, etc. I wanted to have a one-stop shop for all of that. There was also an element of luck. I was at a live book coaching event, and on a lark I pitched one of the three agents who were there. I found a great fit with one of the agents.

What's the most important thing a blogger can do to get noticed in the blogosphere and to build an author platform or fan base?

I'll give a few: quality writing, frequent posting, and a core audience you can find on social media. Groups (on social media sites) are a great place to start.

Network by guest blogging, and comment on others' blog posts. It takes a while to make connections.

Has publishing a book affected your blog, business, or published book in any way?

The paperback had a bigger impact than the e-book did. I can sell at the back of the room when I speak, and it gives me greater credibility.

KARL PALACHUK ON BLOGGING HIS BOOK: *MANAGED SERVICES OPERATIONS MANUAL*

Karl Palachuk's blog, *Small Biz Thoughts* (www.SmallBizThoughts. com), targets technology consultants who focus on small- to medium-sized businesses, or SMB consultants. An early advocate of a business model known in the IT industry as managed services, his first book, *Managed Services in a Month,* grew from a series of long blog posts on that topic. For more than five years the title has been the number one book on Amazon for managed services.

With that success under his belt, he decided to consciously blog a book—*Managed Services Operations Manual: Standard Operating Procedures for Computer Consultants and Managed Service Providers.* This four-volume set of books is the product of a blog post series that lasted over two years.

As part of this book project, Palachuk ran an Indiegogo campaign to raise money for the book. "The idea was to help me fund the book production so that it would come out faster."

Why did you decide to blog a book?

The book I wrote from a blog series was very successful. In fact, it's been the number one hit on Amazon for the term "Managed Services" for five years. So with this project, I knew I wanted to write a longer book series. The problem—as is the case with most authors—is that I also have to do all my other work. The easiest way to make sure I kept up on my blogging as well as made progress on the book was to build a list of topics and blog them one at a time.

Like many bloggers, I like putting out a series of posts to address a topic. This allows me to address something in more detail, and the series keeps readers checking back for the next installment. This works very well for moving material into a book format. In my case, I frequently have very long blog posts. Sometimes one post becomes one chapter. Sometimes it takes two or three posts to become a chapter.

What process did you use to plan out your blogged book?

I started a theme called "SOP Friday" on my blog. *SOP* means "Standard Operating Procedures." The idea was to address one SOP each week. I knew it would be a book when I started, but I didn't realize it would be four books.

How often did you publish posts, and how long did it take you to blog your first draft?

I started the SOP blog series in May 2011. I called it "SOP Friday" so that I would feel the obligation to write a new article every week. I did other blogging as well, but the SOP theme was addressed on Fridays.

It took about three years to complete all the topics I wanted to address in the book. So in the spring of 2014, I started actually laying out the books.

How much new content did you later add to your book? Did you plan for this content in advance (leave it out purposely on the blog), or was it simply added during the editing process?

The book very closely matches the blog content. Approximately 85 percent of the book's content is originally from the blog. The main change, which I didn't really think about while blogging, is that we had to work up fresh graphics for the book. While blogging I simply threw up whatever graphics struck me as interesting at the time. Once we moved to a book format I needed to have better, more consistent graphics.

Once I started compiling the blog posts into a book I needed to write lots of information that connected the individual posts into a unified product.

As a result, the finished four-book set has about 150 pages that were never part of the blog series. That seems like a lot, but it was easy to write a few paragraphs at a time. Plus I added appendices with acronyms and resources for each book.

Do you have some tips you can offer from your experience on how to blog a book?

Make your book blog a project—a major project—in your life and in your business. Talk about it everywhere (Twitter, Facebook, LinkedIn, on the blog, in webinars, etc.). Assuming you've got an audience and you've built a following for the book, talk about it all the time.

This includes building additional websites that support the book in various ways. We bought Google ads to point people to the blog even though we did not have a book to sell. We had other things to sell. And we promised to keep people informed if they signed up for our newsletter.

Getting this four-book set from idea to blog took about two years. Turning it into a physical set of books took about ten months. Much of that ten months was spent promoting and talking about what a cool project it is.

In the final months of the book project, people e-mailed us every day to ask when it would be ready. Our promotional activities created a huge demand.

What did you do that increased your traffic or brought in more unique visitors?

I created a few websites in support of the book project. First, for the Indiegogo campaign we created a site called SOP4SMB.com. This is where we put up information on the campaign while it was live. We also put up the proposed table of contents for the final book series. Once the book was released, this site redirected to the primary book site.

Because the blog posts consisted of whatever topic was on the top of my head at the time, the "book" contents were written out of order. Therefore, it became useful to create an index to the SOP Friday blog series. This was built at Small-BizThoughts.com/Events/SOPFriday.html, and I created another domain to redirect traffic there: SOPFriday.com.

That page became a central source of traffic for the blog. People bookmarked the SOP Friday index and then watched it for changes. Once the book table of contents was complete, I reorganized this site with hyperlinks to all articles in the order they would appear in the book.

Did you see a noticeable increase in traffic when you blogged your book?

My blog has been active since 2006, and I have a pretty good following. So I didn't really see an increase in traffic, but I did see an increase in PR. Because I was blogging regularly about a topic with a specific name—SOP Friday—I was able to use that term in other forums and gain some traction.

I talked about SOP Friday in my newsletter, on Facebook, and even during live presentations. And other people started talking about SOP Friday on LinkedIn, Facebook, and Twitter. So that helped build an audience for the book.

Why did you decide to go the indie route?

I've written a book about this—*Publish Your First Book*. But it basically amounts to one thing: money. As a publisher of nonfiction, I can ask a good price for my books. The set of four books initially sold for a super-sale price of $99. As a self-publisher I got to keep most of that.

Through distribution we keep 60 percent. So no matter what Amazon did with the price, in this case, we got our $59.40 (minus a couple of dollars for production). In the end, we made about $57 per set. When we sold from our own website we made $97 for every $99 sale.

Tell me about your Indiegogo crowdfunding campaign and why you ran it.

We raised just over $13,000 in the fall of 2013 with the goal of getting the book out by summer 2014. As part of the Indiegogo campaign, we also "presold" more than one hundred copies of the book set. The "old" campaign is still up, and you can view it at www.Indiegogo.com/Projects/SOPs-For-The-Successful-Consultant/x/4956392.

We started the Indiegogo campaign when I realized I was closing in on finishing the blog topics I'd set out. We did a lot of research to decide on the length of our campaign. Indiegogo's help files and recommendations are excellent. They give lots of information about how to create a successful campaign.

Do you have any tips for others who want to crowdfund expenses on their blogged books?

If we do this again, the biggest thing we'll do is to start talking about the campaign about a month before we launch it. People tend to pay attention to only a small portion of the social media and newsletters they've subscribed to. As a result, you can run nonstop promotions for a month and only hit a small portion of your audience.

While we had great participation, we also had people telling us for months that they missed the campaign and were sorry they did. The general lesson is: Repeat your message a lot!

What's the most important thing a blogger can do to get noticed in the blogosphere and build an author platform or fan base?

Niche. Niche. Niche. My audience consists of a fairly small universe: small technology consultants who serve small businesses. I don't address government-agency tech support, large consulting companies, or people who support big corporations.

I can say, "I'm one of you. I do this every day." My audience knows me. There are very few people writing and training and speaking in my little niche. As a result, the readers actually feel like they know me. They now pay $279.95 for the four book set and then thank me for producing it!

When we launched the four-book set, we had a super sale of $99—and sold 165 sets in three days. Then it went on sale for $199, and we sold 57 sets over the next month. Finally, the book set moved to its full price of $279.95, and we sell about one set per day from our site.

My point is: We charge a very good price for our book set because it is extremely well focused on a specific market. There are no similar books on the market. There is no competition. That's the power of a niche market.

Has publishing a book affected your blog, business, or published book in any way?

Unlike many bloggers, I actually make my living selling books and materials related to my books. Blogging a book is such a perfect mix of production and promotion that I'm sure I'll do it again.

On one hand, the blog provides free and useful information. On the other hand, it is self-promoting. As you write the blog and help people out, you gain followers and fans. They are eager to help you in return. And that means they are happy to buy your book—knowing full well that they could get 90 percent of it free on your blog.

Do you have any tips regarding the production of the blogged book?

In my case, the drafts of blog posts were stored on my computer, so the blog itself represented the actual finished product for each post. That meant I needed to copy all the posts from the Internet to my local machine. We stumbled onto a great solution for this: www.oDesk.com.

I posted a job request on oDesk. I hired someone to look at my table of contents, copy down the text from each related blog post, and compile the results into one of four Word documents. There were about 150 blog posts in total, and they were definitely not in the same order as the table of contents.

The woman we hired at oDesk accomplished this job in less than a week—and charged us less than $7.00! It was one of the best decisions we could have made. Since then we have hired her to do other work for us as well.

Those four Word documents literally became the first draft of the four-book set.

In addition to your blog, how have you used the Web to promote your blogged-book project?

We put up two pages that helped us drive traffic, attract SEO, and help people use the material from the "book" as I blogged it.

Blogs have one serious drawback for readers: They're in the wrong order. If you're blogging a chronological book, such as a fiction book, then the blog needs to be read backward. If you're blogging a nonfiction book, then the topics might bounce all over the place.

The first page we set up is simply an evolving Table of Contents. I put this page on my regular website. Then I bought the domain SOPFriday.com and pointed that to the table of contents page. That single page became extremely popular—and drove massive traffic to the blog itself. It also became very handy for me to quickly search for previous blog posts and link to them.

Then we created a page just for the book (Managed ServicesOperationsManual.com). There we described the project, posted some PDF files to download, and set up a sales site. That's the page we drive Google advertising to. When people buy the books, they are simply redirected to the shopping cart on our primary bookstore.

PAMELA SLIM ON BOOKING HER BLOG: ESCAPE FROM CUBICLE NATION

Pamela Slim's *Escape from Cubicle Nation* blog, which can be found at www.EscapeFromCubicleNation.com/Pamela-Slims-Blog, provides support, resources, information, and training for corporate employees who aspire to start their own businesses. She started the blog in October 2005, and it was later tapped for a book of the same name by Penguin/Portfolio. *Escape from Cubicle Nation: From Corporate Prisoner to Thriving Entrepreneur* was released in 2009 and contains about 70 percent new content and 30 percent blog posts. Because she wrote a how-to book for readers, Slim says, "There was lots of context I had to wrap around the individual posts that illustrated particular points."

Why did you begin blogging?

I started blogging for the specific purpose of building an online presence and a client base for my business-coaching practice. Prior to starting my blog, I had been a successful consultant to large corporations for ten years, marketing my business primarily with word-of-mouth referrals. I moved to Arizona from the San Francisco Bay Area and got married. Because we knew we wanted to have children, I wanted to shift my business model from in-person consulting, which involved lots of travel, to online coaching and writing. I started my blog when my son was seven months old.

How did you choose your topic?

As a consultant, I worked with thousands of employees and executives from every type of business you could imagine. In every company, regardless of its reputation or financial situation, there were always a few people who would pull me aside and quietly say, "I would love to work for myself, but I have no idea how to do it! Can you help me?" It was always curious to me that they felt starting a business was such a mystery since there were thousands of books and blogs on the subject.

After researching the topic and getting trained by Martha Beck as a life coach, it became clear to me that, while there was tons of information about starting a business, there were very few resources that integrated the stress of personal change with the business journey itself. So I decided to write about the things I knew were on people's minds but that they would probably never admit in public: like how you can get over the fear of telling your spouse you want to quit your job to start a business, or how you can avoid living in a van down by the river if your business plans go awry.

What, if any, market research did you do before beginning your blog?

I did a fair amount of work researching the demographics and psychographics of my target audience by describing their profile in detail and doing lots of keyword searches on terms like "start a business" and "become an entrepreneur" to see what kinds of resources were available. I also looked up lots of popular blogs on Technorati, the most robust directory at the time, to see what best-in-class blogs looked like. Beyond that, I did not do tons of research, since I was passionate about the topic and convinced there was a market for what I wanted to write about.

Did you think you were writing a book, did you plan on blogging a book, or were you simply blogging on your topic? (In retrospect, would doing one or the other have made it easier to later write your book?)

I had no intention of writing a book when I first started my blog. I was writing it to grow my business and to create a body of good online content, so I was quite surprised when publishers began expressing interest in a book. If I had known beforehand that I was working on a book, I think it would have tripped me up because I may have approached it from a more structured perspective instead of writing only about things that I felt passionate about.

How long did it take for you to gain blog readers, and can you pinpoint any certain event that created a tipping point when readership increased noticeably?

It took about a year to develop a steady group of readers. It was very slow at first, but I found great joy in writing so I kept producing posts.

One big tipping point for me was getting featured on venture capitalist and author Guy Kawasaki's blog in May 2006. He was extremely influential in my target market. When he featured my post "An Open Letter to CEOs Across the Corporate World" on his blog (escapefrom cubiclenation.com/2006/05/04/open-letter to-ceos-coos-cios-and-cfos-across-the-corporate-world), traffic and subscribers exploded. After that exposure, my growth was quicker and supported by influencers like Seth Godin, Kathy Sierra, and Hugh MacLeod.

What did you do to drive traffic (readers) to your blog?

My best strategy for drawing traffic to the blog was to continually turn out relevant content for my market. Without this, I don't think I would have the long-standing support

I enjoy today. I also frequently wrote about other authors and bloggers, which led to mutual support, friendship, and connection.

When Twitter and Facebook came on the scene, they helped amplify individual posts and increase my reader base.

Due to the topic of my blog, I got quoted quite a bit in mainstream press like *The New York Times*, *BusinessWeek*, *Fortune*, *Psychology Today*, and *USA Today*. This helped increase my blog's visibility and cement the credibility of my message.

How did your blog-to-book deal come about?

An author friend introduced me to his agent and suggested we work together to outline a book. I worked with the agent for a few months, but we never really gelled; I didn't feel passionate about the outline we had created for the book. I blogged about the experience and told my readers I was going to step back from pursuing a book deal for awhile to focus on writing more on my blog.

About a year later, I got an e-mail from Emily Rapoport, an editor at Penguin, who said, "I read on your blog that you were interested in writing a book. Could we talk about it?" Needless to say, I jumped at the chance, and we started brainstorming ideas. I felt immediate rapport with her, so she introduced me to an agent she had worked with, and we put together a proposal in about three weeks. We turned it in on a Friday and by Tuesday had a signed deal. We had a fantastic working relationship the whole way through the project, so it was especially sweet when our book won Best Small Business/Entrepreneur Book of 2009 from 800 CEO Read.

What advice would you give writers who want to blog a book (and build readership/platform while doing so)?

The best place to try out ideas for a book is on a blog! Don't let yourself get stressed out by book structure or perfect writing. Pay attention to the kinds of things your readers are interested in and experiment often. You will need many more times raw content from your blog than you can fit in your book, so write with abandon.

What's the most important thing a blogger can do to get noticed in the blogosphere?

Write great stuff. In an ever-increasing sea of content, only the really great blogs will get noticed. People will not be passionate about sharing mediocre writing.

Stay humble. Promote other great writers frequently—not to cultivate favors but because you feel that what they have to say will help your readers. Generosity, sharing, and fostering great work will always beat short-term political posturing.

REGGIE SOLOMON ON BOOKING HIS BLOG: *I GARDEN URBAN STYLE*

Reggie Solomon is the creator of two blogs, *Urban Garden Casual* (UrbanGardenCasual.com) and *Tomato Casual* (www.TomatoCasual. com). *Urban Garden Casual* is focused on helping urban dwellers garden, and *Tomato Casual* is focused on everything tomato for people who love the red fruit.

His book, *I Garden Urban Style*, produced with co-author Michael Nolan, is based on his blog *Urban Garden Casual*. The book arms readers with the knowledge they need to get the most satisfying results from their urban-gardening efforts and investment. The book offers instruction on many urban-gardening options, from window gardens to container gardens to herb gardens to community gardens, appealing to a wide variety of people, from those wanting to commit little time and effort to those wanting an active, fulfilling hobby. The book closely resembles the blog but has striking and vivid photography. "We even included article pullouts directly from the blog in the book," says Solomon. "This book definitely feels like my blog, but richer."

Why did you begin blogging?

I began blogging in 2007 as an experiment in engaging emerging media and new ways of working using the Internet. Through the experience of blogging, I learned how to hire people virtually, manage and work with remote teams around the world, and build a customized blog interface without having any technical knowledge, all while assembling specialized knowledge on a couple of niche subjects of interest. Not bad for a side project. Two years after starting my blog, I landed my first book deal.

How did you choose your topic?

Niche is the new black, and so went the subjects covered on my blogs, *Tomato Casual* and *Urban Garden Casual*.

I chose these two niche areas in part because no one else was blogging about them. I began with the goal to assemble the world's largest repository of articles about tomatoes and urban gardening and, especially with the case of tomatoes, I've pretty much done it. I knew that if I could create the most content on these two specialized subjects, the Internet would lead readers to my door, and I could eventually figure out a way to monetize that interest. Producing a book is one of the ways I'm doing that, and I expect other opportunities to emerge in the future.

Tomato Casual is focused on "Everything Tomato for People who Love Tomatoes." We are not only obsessed with growing, eating, and cooking with tomatoes, we're also obsessed with all things tomato whether it be art, music, wallpaper, recipes, or movies. We are passionate about tomatoes.

Urban Garden Casual is focused on "Gardening for the Urban Dweller." We help city dwellers reclaim the pleasures of noncity living within the confines of urban space by bridging traditional gardening with the special needs of urban and small-space gardeners in the modern world. We want to help people be as comfortable gardening as they are shuffling between tracks on their iPods.

With both blogs, I chose to engage my niches with a decidedly "casual" take and built "casual" into the actual branding. We have taken what has largely been written about from a dry and technical perspective and have made it our own by making it casual and thus more accessible.

What, if any, market research did you do before beginning your blog?

A personal interest in growing tomatoes and gardening in the city served as the primary motivation behind the creation of both blogs; however, I did qualify both interests to ensure there was a market for information on both topics.

What's the most popular item grown in an American garden? What item do you find on the cover of most seed magazines and popularly sold at big-box home improvement stores and gardening centers? What item can be inexpensively grown in one's own garden with a taste far superior to that found in stores at premium prices? Yep. Tomatoes!

In the case of urban gardening, I couldn't find any resources that addressed the particular urban gardening interest. Most of the books I read focused on high-end landscaping of small urban spaces, but there were few resources for gardeners like me who were focused on affordable small-space vegetable gardening. I wanted to live more sustainably and reduce my carbon imprint. This growing trend, combined with being a foodie who prizes fresh ingredients, made my focus on urban gardening seem market ready.

Did you think you were writing a book, did you plan on blogging a book, or were you simply blogging on your topic? (In retrospect, would doing one or the other have made it easier to later write your book?)

I outsource most of the content creation of my blogs. It became apparent very quickly after trying to produce content for both blogs myself that my bigger competitive advantage would be in assembling the most information about both niche areas rather than making the blogs solely about my personal perspective and voice. I have two to five writers working for me at any time who create most of the content for my sites.

While I did not begin blogging with the explicit plan to write a book, it did enter my mind from time to time. It was not until a niche hobby-book publisher approached me and asked me if I would be interested in writing a book on urban gardening and submitting a book proposal for their review that I seriously moved the idea from dinner party chatter to action.

Again, my goal when I started both blogs was to assemble the world's largest collection of information on tomatoes and urban gardening and respond to whatever opportunities this brought to my door. The fact that my urban garden blog pops up within the first three results on Google for "urban garden" searches did not go unnoticed by my publisher and is likely how they found me. My blog is a top destination for reaching and marketing to urban gardeners. What better platform from which to launch a niche book?

How long did it take for you to gain blog readers, and can you pinpoint any certain event that created a tipping point when readership increased noticeably?

It took me about two years to build an audience for both blogs. Engaging social networking definitely helped. I opened groups on www.Flickr.com for people to share photos of their urban gardening and tomato adventures and honestly forgot about the group I'd set up. I was utterly surprised in checking my Flickr page a year later to find hundreds of people were submitting photos to my groups regularly. A similar occurrence happened after setting up my Facebook and Twitter pages as well.

I've considered outsourcing the social-networking management of my site, since I know this could be done better. We may all wish for a silver bullet to bolster readership, but it's less a case of scoring a home run and more a case of getting singles on the board. Google PageRank rewards this latter strategy, too.

What did you do to drive traffic (readers) to your blog?

I equipped my sites with tools to help people share content with friends. I've always had buttons that have made it easy to send articles to friends and to share content within popular social networks. Producing good content and hiring enthusiastic writers for my blogs who have communities in which they share content also helped drive traffic to my sites. My blogs have been featured in *The New York Times* and *Fox TV News,* and they have been linked to many other popular periodicals, websites, and publications.

What one or two things that you did would you attribute to your blogging success (and to the book deal you landed)?

Niche focus has been the key to my blogging success. My blogs would not enjoy the traction they do if I didn't serve up fresh, focused content to feed hungry search engines. Having an enthusiastic and talented group of writers and contributors has also been key to the success of my blogs and book. I partnered with one of my writers, Michael Nolan, to produce the book, and we featured the work of many of my other blog contributors. I'm happy the publishing of the book helped my entire writing team become published authors and contributors. The blog has been a product of "we" from the beginning, and so has the book. "We" is how I roll.

What advice would you give to writers who want to blog a book (and build readership/platform while doing so)?

Focus on building quality content. It will be the foundation of your success.

We publish two to three times a week with posts averaging 250 to 500 words. When we occasionally have articles that are longer, we break them up into Part One and Part Two articles. Google eats fresh content for breakfast, lunch, and dinner, so spread out your content as you do your meals. You wouldn't eat all of your food for the week on Monday and not expect to get hungry during the week. The same goes for Google. Feed it and wean it to whatever posting frequency makes sense for you; just be consistent with your publishing schedule so your readers know what to expect.

Building readership is about relationship building. Build relationships through your blog as you would in person. We reached out to many of our early readers and mentioned them in our blog and visited their blogs to comment. It's all about relationships—so easy to build and sometimes easier to squander.

Lastly, think carefully if you want to be published through a traditional publishing channel. Having one's book published through a traditional publisher does earn one a bit of cred, but consider whether long-term earnings from e-book publishing might be more attractive. Self-publishing through an e-book format may prove the most profitable in the long run while giving you maximum control over your creative content.

What's the most important thing a blogger can do to get noticed in the blogosphere?

To get noticed, be noticeable. Not by SEO gaming tricks but by producing content that attracts positive attention to itself. Big media shouts; niche media whispers. The longtail (a.k.a. Chris Anderson[1]) belongs to whisperers. Lucky are we merry band of whisperers.

Also, write more about the topics people come to your blog to find information on. Using a backend blog analytics package, such as Google Analytics or pMetrics, you can easily find the search terms leading people to your site and create more content for users looking for information about that subject or concept. This means you can produce content just as easily from Z to A as you can from A to Z.

And lastly, have fun with it!

---

1. Chris Anderson is the editor in chief of *Wired*. He wrote an article in the magazine titled "The Long Tail," which he expanded on in the book *The Long Tail: Why the Future of Business Is Selling Less of More*.

BRETT MCKAY ON BOOKING HIS BLOG: THE ART OF MANLINESS

The Art of Manliness (www.ArtOfManliness.com) is a 100,000-plus-subscriber blog started in 2008 by Brett McKay and his wife Kate. According to Brett, the blog is dedicated to "reviving the lost art of manliness" and publishes articles on topics like self-improvement, relationships, dressing and grooming, etiquette, health, finance, and "manly" skills. The goal of the site is to help men better themselves in all areas of their lives.

Based on the blog, the book *The Art of Manliness: Classic Skills and Manners for the Modern Man,* was published in October 2009 by HOW Books. Seventy-five percent of the book consists of articles taken from the blog and edited for the book, and 25 percent of the book's content is new material.

Why did you begin blogging?

I began blogging as a hobby in 2006 during my first year of law school. My first blog was called *The Frugal Law Student* (FrugalLawStudent.com), and the focus was on personal finance for those in law school. I had some mild success with it. In 2008, I started *The Art of Manliness*.

How did you choose your topic?

I was tired of the content geared toward men in magazines like *Men's Health* and *GQ*. It was always about the same stuff—six-pack abs, getting chicks, and expensive clothes. *The Art of Manliness* is the men's magazine I've always wanted to read. At the same time, it seemed like twenty-something guys like me were a little adrift and had lost some of the basic skills and knowledge our grandpas knew. I wanted to rediscover the lost manly arts.

What, if any, market research did you do before beginning your blog?

I didn't do any market research. I just wrote about topics that interested me and discovered that lots of other men were interested in the same stuff.

Did you think you were writing a book, did you plan on blogging a book, or were you simply blogging on your topic? (In retrospect, would doing one or the other have made it easier to later write your book?)

I didn't think I was writing a book when I started *The Art of Manliness*. I was simply blogging about my topic. When we started getting more traffic and things picked up, I started to think, *Hey, maybe we can turn this thing into a book.*

How long did it take for you to gain blog readers, and can you pinpoint any certain event that created a tipping point when readership increased noticeably?

The site took off fairly quickly after I started it. The very first post I wrote, "How to Shave Like Your Grandpa," got picked up on Digg.com and www.Reddit.com, which brought in a ton of traffic. (This was back when getting on the front page of Digg was a huge deal.)

What did you do to drive traffic (readers) to your blog?

First, I leveraged the audience I already had built up at *Frugal Law Student*. Right off the bat in the first month of *The Art of Manliness* I was able to score five hundred subscribers.

And then again, the big thing that rocketed our blog to success was getting discovered on social media sites like Digg.com, Delicious.com, and www.Reddit.com. Every week or so one of our posts would hit the front page of those sites and send tens of thousands of visitors to our site in just a few hours. Other big websites would spot our links on Digg or Reddit, link to us, and send more traffic our way. In just five months after starting the blog, we had over ten thousand subscribers.

How did your blog-to-book deal come about?

We actually didn't pitch our book or come up with a book proposal. About five months after we started *The Art of Manliness*, several editors from different publishers e-mailed us wanting to turn our blog into a book. We took a look at the different offers and decided to go with HOW Books. We inked the deal in July 2008 and started on the draft in August. We turned in the completed book in December 2008, and the book was published in October 2009.

What one or two things that you did would you attribute to your blogging success (and to the book deal you landed)?

Identifying an untapped niche was probably the most important thing. There wasn't a magazine out there that appealed to the thousands of men who weren't interested in hot babes and cars and earnestly wanted to learn how to improve their lives and become better men, men who were interested in good, old-fashioned, wholesome manliness. We found success by filling that void.

What advice would you give writers who wanted to blog a book (and build readership/platform while doing so)?

Create a blog that stands out from the thousands of others out there, and work hard to make it popular. Showing publishers you have a big following will make getting a book deal far easier.

What's the most important thing a blogger can do to get noticed in the blogosphere?

I know it's a cliché, but writing interesting, unique, helpful, top-quality content is the key—"evergreen" content that will be just as useful to people five years from now. We set ourselves apart from other sites in that we don't just look at other blogs to get ideas and regurgitate what is already being shared around the Web. Instead, we do a ton of research—we check out lots of books from the library and spend hours poring through them.

Besides quality content creation, be helpful to people in the blogosphere. Link to them on your blog, share their links on Twitter and Facebook, and e-mail them with tips for their own blog. Don't just focus on the big fish either. Focus on the small guys, too.

MARTHA ALDERSON ON BOOKING HER BLOG: *THE PLOT WHISPERER*

Martha Alderson uses her blog, *The Plot Whisperer* (PlotWhisperer. Blogspot.com), as a place for her to unwind after plot consultations with clients and to share plot tips. "Because writing is a very personal activity (as well as a very public activity—after all, a writer's intention is to be read), a certain intimacy forms between my clients and me during plot consultations," she explains. "As a result, I've been able to draw lessons about how stories unfold and to include the lives of the writers with whom I work in my blog."

The Plot Whisperer: Secrets of Story Structure Any Writer Can Master organizes Alderson's blog posts into the ultimate guide to writing page-turning novels, memoirs, and screenplays that sell. It was released by Adams Media in October 2011. Although the rough draft of the book contained about 90 percent blog content, Alderson says, "In the editing process, things shifted and changed so that, though the blog is reflected throughout the book, probably 40 percent is from the blog and 60 percent is new content."

Why did you begin blogging?

I began teaching plot to writers when writers' websites were still a rarity and mostly static. When blogs came along, I loved how easy it was to offer updated information, receive nearly instantaneous feedback, and remain interactive with visitors.

How did you choose your topic?

I hang up the phone or turn off Skype after a plot consultation and invariably continue to mull over insights I gleaned and impressions I was struck with. Often, relevant information bubbles to the surface, and rather than allow the insight or feedback or wisdom to languish, I choose instead to share on my blog what I learn with and from other writers.

What, if any, market research did you do before beginning your blog?

It never even occurred to me to do market research.

Did you think you were writing a book, did you plan on blogging a book, or were you simply blogging on your topic?

I was simply blogging about plot.

How long did it take for you to gain blog readers, and can you pinpoint any certain event that created a tipping point when readership increased noticeably?

As soon as other writers started blogging about the help I provided them through my first book, *Blockbuster Plots Pure & Simple*, plot consultations, conferences, workshops, and retreats, my readership began growing. Writer's blogs and websites bigger than mine, like *The Daily Coyote*, The Writers Store, and NaNoWriMo (National Novel Writing Month), started linking to my website and continue to send writers to the *Plot Whisperer* blog today. *Writer's Digest* magazine awarded the *Plot Whisperer* blog the honor of a spot as one of the 101 Best Websites for Writers for three years running and directs new visitors to the blog each year.

What did you do to drive traffic (readers) to your blog?

I use my website, Blockbuster Plots for Writers, as well as Facebook, Twitter, LinkedIn, Goodreads, and my blog *How Do I Plot a Novel, Memoir, Screenplay?*

I strive monthly to send out a free plot tips e-zine to subscribers and pack it with plot support. The e-zine always has a link to the most recent blog post and is a terrific way to stay in touch with writers who know me or know of my work.

I find different demographics prefer different modes of keeping in touch; thus I attempt to cast out the broadest reach I can—using Twitter, YouTube, my blog, my website, and Facebook to send out plot tips, inspiration, and support to writers all over the world.

How did your blog-to-book deal come about?

My agent was pitching a second edition of *Blockbuster Plots Pure & Simple*, and instead Paula Munier, acquisitions editor for Adams Media, asked me to write *The Plot Whisperer* book based on my blog.

What one or two things that you did would you attribute to your blogging success (and to the book deal you landed)?

My deepest intention always has been to share useful information with writers. Writing a story from beginning to end is no easy feat. I wish to help other writers achieve their dreams of completing a worthy project. During a plot consultation, I try to reawaken in writers the rhythm of the Universal Story form. Stories reflect the heartbeat of the universe. Writers and readers, all of us, pulse to this universal rhythm. I think the exploration of universal truths through my blog inspires writers—and blog readers.

What advice would you give writers who wanted to blog a book (and build readership/platform while doing so)?

Write your passion. Always consider your visitors. Update your blog consistently.

What's the most important thing a blogger can do to get noticed in the blogosphere?

Share valuable information that is true and authentic to you.

CHRISTIAN LANDER ON BOOKING HIS BLOG: *STUFF WHITE PEOPLE LIKE*

Christian Lander reportedly received a $350,000 advance from Random House Trade Paperbacks to turn his blog, *Stuff White People Like* (StuffWhitePeopleLike.com), into a book, *Stuff White People Like: The Definitive Guide to the Unique Taste of Millions.* Lander says, "The blog and the book are both a comedic guide to white people." The book consists of 50 percent new material including charts, graphs, and other work from graphic designers.

Why did you begin blogging?

I started blogging to entertain my friends. I have a group of buddies who I think are hilarious, and we are always trying to make each other laugh. Since I can't be in the same city as them, I found that writing was a fun way to keep them entertained. There isn't really anything in the world I enjoy more than making people laugh.

How did you choose your topic?

My friend Myles and I were talking about the TV show *The Wire,* and Myles said he didn't trust any white person who didn't watch the show. So we started guessing what these people were doing instead of watching *The Wire,* and we came up with things like yoga, getting divorced, and having gifted kids. Then I said, "It's blog time," and started writing to make him laugh.

What, if any, market research did you do before beginning your blog?

Absolutely nothing. I started the blog to make my friends laugh; all of the success has been a by-product.

Did you think you were writing a book, did you plan on blogging a book, or were you simply blogging on your topic?

I was blogging only to make my friends laugh. I had no idea the blog could become a book, and this was back in

2008 when publishing had really cooled off on blog-to-book deals.

How long did it take for you to gain blog readers, and can you pinpoint any certain event that created a tipping point when readership increased noticeably?

It took about three weeks to go from one hundred hits a day to thirty thousand hits a day. From there it blew up to hundreds of thousands of hits. The day it exploded was the day it was featured on Comedy Central's *Insider*. Truthfully, the traffic from major media outlets was nice, but sites like www.StumbleUpon.com always added more traffic than any traditional media source. So while big media can start the spark, it's people sharing the posts over social media that causes a blog to really grow.

What did you do to drive traffic (readers) to your blog?

I kept writing. I know that sounds obnoxious, but it's true. I didn't try to change anything. I figured I was successful because I offered people a laugh, so trying to do anything to change that seemed foolish. Also, I agreed to do every single interview request that came through the site: blogs, student papers, podcasts, all of it.

How did your blog-to-book deal come about?

The site became very, very popular, and literary agents started contacting me. That was it.

What one or two things that you did would you attribute to your blogging success (and to the book deal you landed)?

Luck. Luck more than anything. The truth is that success is only partially merit based. I was lucky enough to write on a topic that came along at exactly the right time in terms of publishing, the Internet, and America's willingness to think about race and class.

Also, I think that people could see I was writing because I loved it and that the blog wasn't set up to try to make the readers do all the work. What I mean by that is a lot of people write blogs and then expect their friends and readers to share them with everyone and do the work of promotion. The truth is that if your blog is good enough and connects with enough people, they will share it on their own. You can't have your readers do your work for you. You have to make it so good and so compelling that readers have no choice but to forward it on.

What advice would you give writers wanting to blog a book (and build readership/platform while doing so)?

Don't do it. Blog because you love it. Blog because you're a writer who needs to exercise his ability to write. Do not go into this with dollar signs in your eyes or else everyone who reads your blog will see right through you.

Also, when it comes to readers and comments, do not take the negative ones personally. Do your best to ignore them; the energy required to convert someone who already dislikes you is not repaid. Just accept that no one is liked by everyone, and embrace the people who like what you do.

What's the most important thing a blogger can do to get noticed in the blogosphere?

Be good, and remember that success is not a sign of your skill as a writer. If John Milton had a blog today no one would read it. Success is based partially on talent but mostly on an ability to connect with a broad audience. So when it comes to getting noticed you have to have an original idea you execute well.

Also the "Hollywood system" is a good one for blogging. Can you tell me what your blog is about in a sentence? If you can't, it probably isn't going to be broadly popular.

CONCLUSION

HOW THE *HOW TO BLOG A BOOK* BLOG GOT PUBLISHED

I began the *How to Blog a Book* blog in February 2009. I completed the whole book before the end of June 2010—just five months later.

So what happened to the blogged book when I finished? At first I blogged sporadically, relieved to be done with that first draft. I began posting blogs to *How to Blog a Book* only when I thought of it, maybe once a week, a few times a month, when I saw a blog-to-book success story or I heard a bit of interesting blogging or publishing news. I didn't want to let the blog die, but I also did not want to devote a ton of time to it. I had four other blogs that needed my attention.

After a few months, I noticed traffic dropping off. I realized I'd made a big mistake by discontinuing regular publishing of posts to the *How to Blog a Book* blog. So I created a blogging plan and schedule, and I began posting to the blog twice a week. I've continued doing so ever since, and its unique visitors, number of page views, and subscriber count continues to grow. (Interestingly, this blog has the lowest bounce rate of all my blogs—below 5 percent consistently, according to Google Analytics.)

In September 2010, I began working on a proposal. As soon as my agent heard I had finished blogging the book, she encouraged me to send her a proposal so she could start marketing the book to publishers. In mid-November, I sent her a final version, which she submitted to several publishers. We revised the *How to Blog a Book* proposal in January and again in February 2011 after receiving a few rejections. She then sent it to Writer's Digest Books. In March we revised the proposal once more and re-sent it to Writer's Digest—to the same acquisitions editor, whom we had not heard from yet.

During this time, I kept reiterating to my agent that I wanted to get the book out quickly. I wanted to be first to market with the idea. I told her I would self-publish if need be, and I began editing the manuscript and thinking about a design for the book's cover.

In early July I heard the good news that the acquisitions editor and the publisher at Writer's Digest Books had accepted the book—if I would agree to write 10,000 words more than I had proposed. Of course, I agreed. (I'm a very verbose writer. Writing too little is never a problem for me.) I was told the proposal would be presented to the sales and marketing team just a week or two later. So we waited again. Then my agent got the call that the book had been accepted. Woo-hoo!

However, since Writer's Digest Books also wanted to be first to market, I was given a deadline just eight weeks out from the time the book was accepted. I was planning to be away one of those weeks at a conference, and three and a half of the weeks I would be in New York City with my son. I'd be working, but only for a few hours per day. That meant I had three weeks to get the manuscript edited and revised and make any additions, including the two chapters that weren't written. Also, one of the chapters involved inviting contributors to participate, and if they didn't agree, I might not meet my deadline. I had my work cut out for me.

When I received the actual contract two weeks after I returned home from the conference, the deadlines had changed. I had to turn in just one-quarter of the manuscript before I left for New York, and I had two more months to turn in the rest. Too late. As I put my signature on the contract, I'd already completed the entire book except the chapter that required contributors. This I would turn in when I returned from New York about a month and half later.

Just seven months after sending in the final chapter, I held a bound and printed copy of *How to Blog a Book* in my hands—proof that the concept presented in my blogged book really does work. If you take a great idea, produce and carry out a strong business plan, and build a great platform on the Internet by blogging your book and driving traffic to that blog, you can land a traditional publishing deal.

If I can do it, so can you.

The story doesn't end there, though. *How to Blog a Book* earned back its advance in under six months, which means it sold enough copies to cover the money paid to me by the publisher to write the book. (An author's advance from a publisher is based on predicted sales of a book; today, the majority of books never earn back their advance. If a book earns back its advance in a year or less, it is considered successful.) It also went on to a second printing early in the third quarter of its first year in print—another indication of its high sales.

Also, upon release, *How to Blog a Book* made it to the Amazon Top 100 list in all three of the categories in which it is listed, and it has stayed there. It's a rare day when I don't find it on at least one Amazon bestseller list. That means it remained an Amazon bestseller since 2012.

I'll say it again: If I can do it, so can you—traditionally or independently, blogged or booked, whichever you choose.

There's no time like now to be a writer, a blogger, or an author. The publishing industry is an exciting place to hang your hats—your business and your writer hats, your publisher and your blogger hats. But don't just hang them up—put them on! Do the work and get your book blogged and published. I hope this inspires you to sit down at your computer and start blogging your book (if you haven't already).

If you do, you can join the ranks of the many blog-to-book success stories being made. These bloggers landed traditional publishing deals in recent years—and I've included their websites so you can check them out and get inspired.

- Jennifer Fulwiler's *Something Other than God* (www.ConversionDiary.com)
- Jessica Hagy's *How to Be Interesting (in 10 Simple Steps)* (ThisIsIndexed.com)
- Phil Edward's *Fake Science 101: A Less-Than-Factual Guide to Our Amazing World* (FakeScience.org)
- Joakim Christoffersson's *Nano Workouts* (NanoWorkout.com)

- Madeleine Roux's *Allison Hewitt Is Trapped* (HelpTheyAre Coming.WordPress.com)
- Gina Sheridan's *I Work at a Public Library* (IWorkAtAPublicLibrary.com)

Here's my challenge to you: Blog a book in a year or less. How? Easy. A blog post a day is a book—or two—a year. Think about it: 360 posts multiplied by 300 words equals 108,000 words. That's easily two non-fiction books, a memoir, or a long novel. I challenge you to begin writing a blog post a day and to set a goal to finish blogging a book in a year ... or less—and, of course, to get discovered (or at least published) in the process.

Good luck!

ABOUT THE AUTHOR

Nina Amir, the best-selling author of *The Author Training Manual*, is a speaker, a blogger, and an author, book, and blog-to-book coach. Known as the Inspiration to Creation Coach, she helps creative people combine their passion and purpose so they move from idea to inspired action and positively and meaningfully impact the world as writers, bloggers, authorpreneurs, and blogpreneurs.

Some of Amir's clients have sold 300,000+ copies of their books, landed deals with major publishing houses, and created thriving businesses around their books. She is the founder of National Nonfiction Writing Month, a.k.a. the Write Nonfiction in November Challenge, and the Nonfiction Writers' University.

Amir maintains four blogs, guest posts for other bloggers, and constantly blogs books (and books blogs) of all lengths, such as *Authopreneur, Blogpreneur, The Nonfiction Book Proposal Demystified, Blogging Basics for Aspiring Authors*, and *The Nonfiction NOW! Guide to Writing a Book in 30 Days*, most of which are Amazon Top 100 bestsellers. As many as four of her books have appeared on the same Amazon bestseller list at the same time.

She holds a BA in magazine journalism with a concentration in psychology and lives in the Santa Cruz Mountains above Los Gatos, California.

Find out more about her at NinaAmir.com.

INDEX